הגדה בכל דור ודור

Haggadah B'chol Dor Va-Dor

A Haggadah for all Generations

וְהִגַּדְתָּ לְבִנְךָ

... and you shall tell it to your children

London
2010/5770

Introduction

A Children's *Seder*

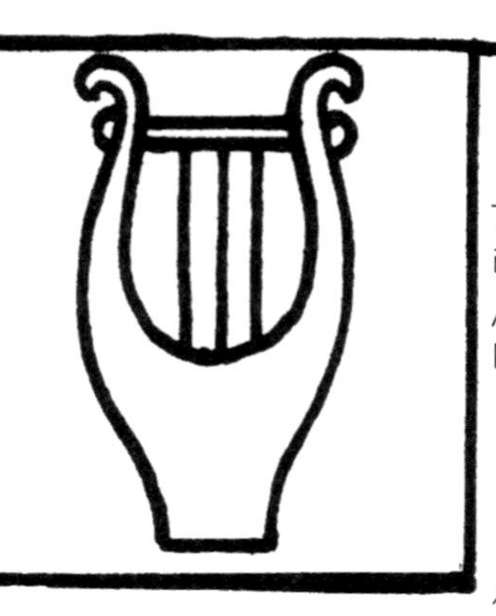

The *Pesach Seder* fulfils a simple yet profound biblical instruction. In Exodus chapter 13, we read:

And you shall tell your child on that day 'This is what the Eternal One did for me when bringing me out of Egypt'.

וְהִגַּדְתָּ לְבִנְךָ בַּיּוֹם הַהוּא לֵאמֹר
בַּעֲבוּר זֶה עָשָׂה יְהוָֹה לִי בְּצֵאתִי מִמִּצְרָיִם.

V'higgad'ta l'vin'cha ba-yom ha-hu leimor ba'avur zeh asah Adonai li b'tzeiti mi-mitzrayim.

This emphasises the two most important elements of the *Seder*. Firstly, it is meant to be told to our children. As such, it is important that it is presented to them in a way that is memorable, and encourages them to consider the significance of the events that led to our ancestors gaining their freedom from slavery in Egypt.

Secondly, this verse reminds us that the struggle for freedom is an ongoing task that is the responsibility of every generation of Jews. The statement 'This is what the Eternal One did for **me**' makes clear that this is not some ancient event from which we are separated by many centuries but a challenge and a responsibility to be faced by every generation of Jews. A *Seder* is not a successful or even a legitimate *Seder* if it does not speak to the next generation and remind them of their duty to remember their ancestors and to carry the *Pesach* message of liberty for all in their consciousness as bearers of the message of Judaism.

In order to ensure that the lessons of the *Seder* are made accessible to our children, the following pages are offered as an alternative *Haggadah*. On the left-hand pages are readings that will hopefully be suitable for those children who are just learning to read. The right-hand pages are for more advanced readers. The subject matter on each facing page is the same, meaning that the two pages can be read in tandem by readers of differing ages and abilities. At the foot of each right-hand page is a reference to the pages in the main *Haggadah* that deal with similar material so it is possible to incorporate the different versions of this *Haggadah* in a single *Seder*. At all stages of the *Seder*, children – and indeed all participants – should be encouraged to discuss and ask questions about what is happening.

As a rough estimate, reading the left-hand pages of this children's *Haggadah* will take around twenty minutes; the right-hand pages perhaps half an hour. If, in that time, the participants gain an awareness of the experiences and the courage of their ancestors, their duty to recall those experiences and to spread the message of liberty that was learned from them, then you will have fulfilled your responsibility to pass the message of *Pesach* to the next generation.

Have a happy *Pesach*!

Our *Seder* starts here

Remember...

...that more than three thousand years ago, on this very night, some brave people – our people decided to escape from years of slavery. They wanted to end the suffering they had experienced, they wanted a better future for their children. For longer than they could remember, they had been slaves, as had their parents and grandparents. But now, suddenly, they had a chance to escape.

What lay ahead of them was a wilderness, a frightening place. But it was also the way to freedom. If they did not take this opportunity to run from this place of oppression, they, and those who came after them, would be slaves for ever.

So they left. Taking with them what little food they could carry, they gathered up their children and led them into the desert. Behind them was a life of slavery and suffering. In front of them, a wilderness and a future of freedom. When they left, they did not know if they would live or die. They did not know that they were actually the first generation of what history would eventually call the Jewish people. They did not know that what they were doing would be written in a book that would be called the Torah, would be remembered and recalled in every generation at this season, with this ceremony, this meal we call the *Seder*.

That is why we are here this evening. To remember the courage of our people who left Egypt on this night hundreds of years ago. To remember the people who have remembered throughout the generations as we do tonight. To understand our connection with our past and our responsibility to our future.

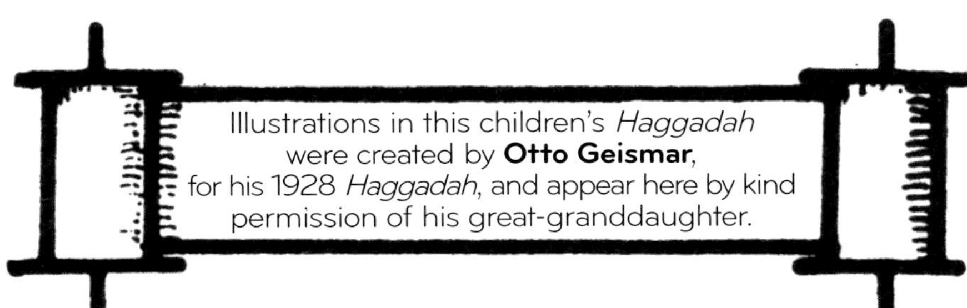

Kiddush

Leader:
Welcome to our *Seder*. This celebration is to remind us that our people were slaves in Egypt but they became free. It is a special day for us and we start our special day by lighting candles and making *Kiddush*.

All: We welcome this festival by lighting candles:

The candles are lit

Baruch atah Adonai eloheinu melech ha-olam asher kidd'shanu b'mitzvotav v'tzivvanu l'hadlik ner shel (shabbat v'shel) yom tov.

We thank You God, for Your rules that make us special and for asking us to light the (Sabbath and) festival candles.

All: We welcome this festival by drinking wine or grape juice and giving thanks to God for bringing us joy:

Baruch atah Adonai eloheinu melech ha-olam borei p'ri ha-gafen.

We thank You God, for making the fruit of the vine.

All: We give thanks to God for letting us share this special time together.

Baruch atah Adonai eloheinu melech ha-olam she-hecheyanu v'kiyy'manu v'higgiy'anu la-z'man ha-zeh.

We thank You God, for keeping us alive, looking after us, and letting us share this special time.

The first glass of wine or grape juice is drunk, leaning to the left

קִדּוּשׁ

Every day should be celebrated because we are so lucky to be alive. Judaism has special days, which we sometimes call 'holy'. On these days we remember things about our past and remind ourselves how being part of the Jewish people makes us feel. Whenever we start a special day, we welcome it by lighting candles.

The candles are lit

בָּרוּךְ אַתָּה יְיָ אֱלֹהֵינוּ מֶלֶךְ הָעוֹלָם, אֲשֶׁר קִדְּשָׁנוּ בְּמִצְוֹתָיו,
וְצִוָּנוּ לְהַדְלִיק נֵר שֶׁל (שַׁבָּת וְשֶׁל) יוֹם טוֹב.

As well as lighting candles, we also drink wine or grape juice. This is another way of reminding ourselves that this is a special day – grapes and the drinks that are made from them have always been used for celebrating times of joy. At our *Seder*, we will drink four glasses. We use the first to welcome this festival:

בָּרוּךְ אַתָּה יְיָ אֱלֹהֵינוּ מֶלֶךְ הָעוֹלָם, בּוֹרֵא פְּרִי הַגָּפֶן.

The *Seder* meal we share to welcome this festival of *Pesach* is an occasion for families to be together. As we look around the table at the people sharing this special time, let us give thanks to God for enabling us to be together:

בָּרוּךְ אַתָּה יְיָ אֱלֹהֵינוּ מֶלֶךְ הָעוֹלָם, שֶׁהֶחֱיָנוּ וְקִיְּמָנוּ וְהִגִּיעָנוּ
לַזְּמַן הַזֶּה.

We praise You, Eternal God, Ruler of the universe, for keeping us alive, sustaining us, and enabling us to reach this season.

The first glass of wine or grape juice is drunk, leaning to the left (pages 2,3,4)

Karpas

Leader:
To help us remember this special day, we have many different things on the table.

Let's begin with the *Karpas*, parsley, a green herb which tells us that spring is here.

Baruch atah Adonai eloheinu melech ha-olam borei p'ri ha-adamah.

We thank You God, for making food grow from the ground.

All take a piece of parsley, dip it in salt water and eat it.

כַּרְפַּס

Another name for *Pesach* is *chag ha-aviv* – the spring festival. All around us we see the world coming back to life after the winter. Hundreds of years ago, our ancestors did not have warm homes. Winter was a difficult time for them. So they were very pleased when the first signs of spring appeared – and when the first full moon of the spring was in the sky, they held a spring festival.

To remember this, and to give our thanks for the world coming back to life at this time of year, we eat Karpas, some green herbs.

בָּרוּךְ אַתָּה יְיָ אֱלֹהֵינוּ מֶלֶךְ הָעוֹלָם, בּוֹרֵא פְּרִי הָאֲדָמָה.

We thank You, Eternal God, Ruler of the universe, for making food grow from the ground.

All take a piece of parsley, dip it in salt water and eat it.

Lachma

Refill the glasses with wine or grape juice

Leader:
This is *Matzah*. It is a special type of bread. We eat it at *Pesach* to remind us of how our people suffered when they were slaves in Egypt.

At this point, the leader holds up the three *Matzot*.
The middle one is broken in two and the larger piece is the *Afikoman*,
which will later be hidden to allow the children to search for it.

All:
This is *Matzah*. When we eat it let us remember how lucky we are not to be slaves and promise to help the poor people in our world.

לַחְמָא

Refill the glasses with wine or grape juice

Another name for *Pesach* is *chag ha-matzot* – the festival of unleavened bread. *Matzah* is known as *lachma anya* – the 'bread of suffering' – so we eat *Matzah* during *Pesach* to remind us of how hard life was for our ancestors when they were slaves.

This traditional reading reminds us that we should always care for those less fortunate than ourselves and share whatever we have with those who need it.

The middle *Matzah* is broken in two; the larger piece will be hidden as the *Afikoman*. The smaller piece is replaced and the *Matzot* are lifted as we read:

Ha lachma anya di achalu	הָא לַחְמָא עַנְיָא דִּי אֲכַלוּ
av'hatana b'ar'ah d'mitzrayim.	אַבְהָתַנָא בְּאַרְעָא דְמִצְרָיִם.
Kol dich'fin yeiy'tei v'yeichul	כָּל־דִּכְפִין יֵיתֵי וְיֵכֻל,
Kol ditz'rich yeiy'tei v'yif'sach.	כָּל־דִּצְרִיךְ יֵיתֵי וְיִפְסַח.
Ha-shata hacha –	הָשַׁתָּא הָכָא,
l'shata d'atya b'ar'ah d'yisra'el	לְשַׁתָּא דְאַתְיָא בְּאַרְעָא דְיִשְׂרָאֵל.
Ha-shata avdei –	הָשַׁתָּא עַבְדֵי,
l'shata d'atya b'nei chorin	לְשַׁתָּא דְאַתְיָא בְּנֵי חוֹרִין.

This is the bread of affliction our ancestors ate in the land of Egypt. Let all who are hungry come and eat; let all who are in need come and share our Passover. This year here, next year in the land of Israel; this year oppressed, next year free.

(page 6)

Mah nishtanah

Why is this night different...

Leader:

Mah nishtanah ha-lailah ha-zeh mi-kol ha-leilot!

How different this night is from all other nights!

So many special things on our *Seder* table! All these things are here to make us ask questions. Here are some questions to ask:

Mah nishtanah ha-lailah ha-zeh mi-kol ha-leilot!

She-b'chol ha-leilot anu ochlin chameitz u-matzah, ha-lailah ha-zeh kulo matzah?

She-b'chol ha-leilot anu ochlin sh'ar y'rakot, ha-lailah ha-zeh maror?

She-b'chol ha-leilot ein anu matbilin afilu pa'am achat, ha-lailah ha-zeh sh'tei f'amim?

She-b'chol ha-leilot anu ochlin bein yoshvin u-vein m'subin, ha-lailah ha-zeh kullanu m'subin?

On all other nights we eat either leavened or unleavened bread...
On all other nights we eat different types of herbs and vegetables...
On all other nights we do not even dip once...
On all other nights we eat either sitting or leaning...

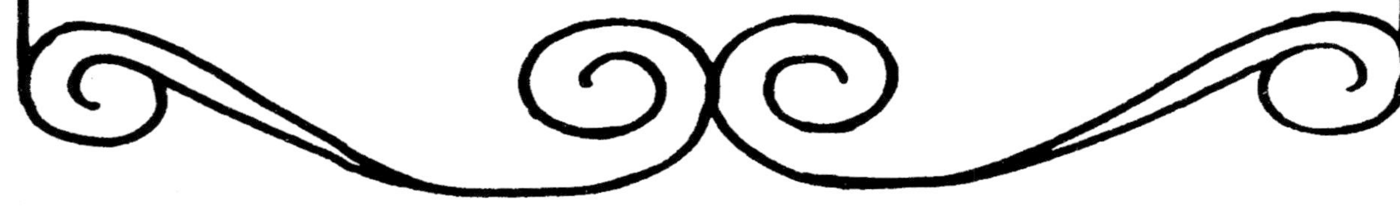

מַה נִּשְׁתַּנָּה

...from all other nights?

Remember that the whole point of the *Seder* is to teach the children about what happened at *Pesach* – 'You shall tell your child on that day...' On the table there are many unusual things, to encourage the children to ask questions all the way through the *Seder*. Just to start them off, here are four questions about this meal. These are traditionally read or sung by the youngest person at the table who is able to do so.

מַה נִּשְׁתַּנָּה הַלַּיְלָה הַזֶּה מִכָּל הַלֵּילוֹת!

שֶׁבְּכָל הַלֵּילוֹת אָנוּ אוֹכְלִין חָמֵץ וּמַצָּה, הַלַּיְלָה הַזֶּה כֻּלּוֹ מַצָּה?

שֶׁבְּכָל הַלֵּילוֹת אָנוּ אוֹכְלִין שְׁאָר יְרָקוֹת, הַלַּיְלָה הַזֶּה מָרוֹר?

שֶׁבְּכָל הַלֵּילוֹת אֵין אָנוּ מַטְבִּילִין אֲפִילוּ פַּעַם אֶחָת,
הַלַּיְלָה הַזֶּה שְׁתֵּי פְעָמִים?

שֶׁבְּכָל הַלֵּילוֹת אָנוּ אוֹכְלִין בֵּין יוֹשְׁבִין וּבֵין מְסֻבִּין,
הַלַּיְלָה הַזֶּה כֻּלָּנוּ מְסֻבִּין?

...why only unleavened bread tonight?
...why bitter herbs tonight?
...why do we dip twice tonight?
...why do we all lean tonight?

Telling the story

Leader:
Who has questions about any of the other the things on the table or what's happening tonight? All these things on the table, this special meal and this festival are meant to help us think about what happened to our people hundreds of years ago when they were slaves in Egypt. Who knows the story of what happened?

Reader 1: Our people were slaves in Egypt.

Reader 2: The Egyptians made them work hard.

Reader 3: Our people were treated very badly and were miserable.

Reader 4: The Egyptians were cruel to them and beat them.

Reader 5: God does not like people to be cruel to other people.

Reader 6: So God decided to rescue our people from Egypt.

Reader 7: God forced Pharaoh the king of Egypt to let the people go.

Reader 8: And so we left Egypt and discovered freedom.

All: That's why we celebrate this festival of *Pesach*!

הַגָּדָה

We are here to remember our ancestors who left Egypt on this night hundreds of years ago. That is the answer to the children's questions in the *Mah Nishtanah*, that is the whole point of this *Seder* and this festival. Here's a poem that tells us what happened in Egypt all those years ago...

On a night just like this in a dark distant land
A people – our people – did what God had planned.
Men, women and children, all of them so brave:
Each knew that no longer would they be a slave.

For so many years they had worked without end
And Pharaoh's taskmasters whipped them again and again.
They built cities for Pharaoh, using bricks without straw
And knew that they couldn't take this any more.

Then Moses showed up with God's sign for the Jews
That came from a bush to Moses with no shoes.
God's message was clear; Moses went to Pharaoh
And told him directly: 'Let my people go!'

Pharaoh flatly refused – which is hardly surprising,
He would never put up with Israel's uprising.
So Moses responded by doing God's bidding:
Promised terrible plagues – and he sure wasn't kidding!

Now the Israelites watched these events with great awe
They had never seen anything like it before
Blood, frogs and darkness, a fiery hail shower –
They knew they were witnessing God's mighty power!

Moses made one final call to the palace front door
And said to Pharaoh 'You won't see me any more:
We'll be leaving when darkness descends at midnight
And when you awake, you will get a big fright.'

The Egyptians awoke and they wailed and they cried
To discover that all of their firstborn had died.
The Israelites packed up, made *Matzah* and left
And Pharaoh just sat there, alone and bereft.

And on this special day we have gathered to tell
The *Haggadah*'s story that we know so well,
The words of our history. And why do we read them?
To recall how our ancestors discovered freedom.

(page 11, 12, 13)

Dayyeinu

Leader:

The Bible tells the story of how ten terrible things, called plagues, struck the Egyptians and made them let our people go free. Let's say those plagues out loud and spill a drop of our drink for each one, like a tear for the suffering caused by these plagues:

Blood

Frogs

Lice

Flies

Cattle disease

Boils

Hail

Locusts

Darkness

Death of the firstborn

Leader:

How lucky we are that God did all these things to save us! And after that, God gave us Shabbat, the Torah, the Prophets and then told us that we should make the world a better place. Even one of those gifts would have been enough...

All:

Dayyeinu!

דַּיֵּנוּ

We are happy that our people escaped from the cruel Egyptians. But in order for this to happen, the Egyptians experienced terrible plagues. As we say each of the plagues, we spill a drop of wine, because even though we are celebrating our people's freedom, we are sorry that others had to suffer.

דָּם	*Dam*
צְפַרְדֵּעַ	*Tz'farde'a*
כִּנִּים	*Kinim*
עָרוֹב	*A'rov*
דֶּבֶר	*Dever*
שְׁחִין	*Sh'chin*
בָּרָד	*Barad*
אַרְבֶּה	*Ar'beh*
חוֹשֶׁךְ	*Choshech*
מַכַּת בְּכוֹרוֹת	*Makkat b'chorot*

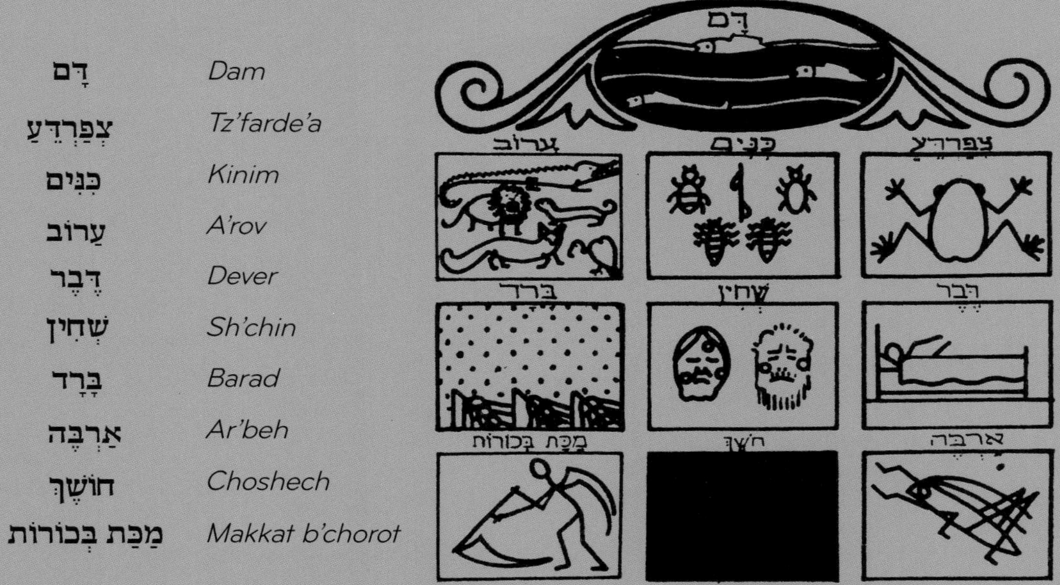

Many are the things that God did for our ancestors! Even if God had done only one of these things, it would still have been enough – דַּיֵּנוּ!

If God had brought us out of Egypt and not given us Shabbat – דַּיֵּנוּ!

If God had given us Shabbat and not given us the Torah – דַּיֵּנוּ!

If God had given us the Torah and not given us the Prophets – דַּיֵּנוּ!

If God had given us the Prophets and not encouraged us to perfect the world – דַּיֵּנוּ!

(pages 14, 15, 16, 17)

הגדה בכל דור ודור

Haggadah B'chol Dor Va-Dor

A Haggadah for all Generations

Edited by

Rabbi Dr Andrew Goldstein

and

Rabbi Pete Tobias

Designed by

Tammy Kustow

Dedicated to

Rabbi Dr Sidney Brichto

1936-2009

London
2010/5770

Acknowledgements

First and foremost, we must acknowledge our debt to Tammy Kustow, whose skill and patience as our designer are worthy of more recognition than will be gained by these few words. Thanks also to members of Liberal Judaism's Rabbinic Conference who offered suggestions and advice; in particular Rabbis Rachel Benjamin, Janet Burden, David Goldberg and Mark Solomon. Ann and Bob Kirk made valuable suggestions on the content and at the proof reading stage.

Our thanks are also due to the numerous contributors to this *Haggadah* for their artwork, poetry and other material. Full details can be found in the notes on the Liberal Judaism website (www.liberaljudaism.org/haggadah).

We would particularly like to thank Joe Buchwald Gelles at haggadahsrus.com and Noam Zion of Zion Holiday Publications inc. from whose concept of telling the story of *Pesach* ever anew, *Haggadah B'chol Dor Va-Dor* draws its own inspiration. Every effort was made to gain permission to use the variety of material such *Haggadot* depend on to represent and transmit the breadth of Jewish experience of Pesach; if we have failed, it was not through lack of effort; please do contact us and we shall be pleased to set matters right.

And finally we would like to thank our wives, Sharon and Robbie, for their patience with us during the lengthy gestation process of this *Haggadah*, during which our respective homes were cluttered with numerous *Haggadot* over which we pored for many hours and days.

Rabbi Dr Andrew Goldstein and Rabbi Pete Tobias

Thanks to the following whose contributions in memory of Rabbi Dr Sidney Brichto have helped to defray the cost of the publication of this *Haggadah:*
Barbara and Stanley Fink, Rosita Rosenberg, William and Jo Kessler, Clive Winston, Phil and Sue Pollock, Rosemary and Walter Goldsmith, Alan Banes, Rabbi Danny Rich, Rabbi Dr David J Goldberg, Rabbi Frank Hellner and Mrs Valerie Boyd-Hellner, Rabbi Andrew and Sharon Goldstein, Rabbi Aaron and Tammy Goldstein, Lucian Hudson, Rabbi Harry and Rose Jacobi, Herefordshire Jewish Community, Northwood & Pinner Liberal Synagogue, The Liberal Synagogue Elstree.

Introduction

Pesach

The origins of *Pesach* are to be found far back in antiquity, in two separate but connected spring festivals: a pastoral celebration by shepherds of the lambing season, and an agricultural celebration by farmers of the year's first grain harvest. This dual connection with nature is reflected in the festival's two earliest names: *Chag ha-Pesach* – the Festival of the Paschal Lamb, and *Chag ha-Matzot* – the Festival of Unleavened Bread.

Some time after the Exodus from Egypt, which most scholars date in the 13th century BCE, these two nature celebrations were unified in a single festival and their meaning reinterpreted religiously, in the light of the most significant event in Jewish history, the Exodus. Thus the word *Pesach* (its root comes from the verb 'to skip', as in the gambolling of new-born lambs) was explained by reference to the last of the Ten Plagues when God 'passed over' *(pasach)* and spared the houses of the Israelites (Exodus 12:23); and the unleavened bread was attributed to the haste of their departure from Egypt (Exodus 12:39). This combined festival, henceforth always called *Pesach*, invariably has the words *z'man cheiruteinu* – The Season of our Freedom – appended to it in all prayers and blessings.

Over the course of the centuries, the observance of *Pesach* developed four complementary strands of meaning. First, it celebrates the springtime re-awakening of nature; second, it commemorates the momentous deliverance that gave birth to the Israelite people; third, it proclaims freedom as a supreme Jewish value; and finally, it looks forward to the Messianic Age of redemption, when all who are oppressed will know freedom.

The *Seder*

From earliest times, *Pesach* was an occasion not only for public worship, but also for a more intimate celebration by families or groups of families and friends. This took the form of a festive meal in which a lamb was eaten together with bitter herbs and unleavened bread (Exodus 12:8). After the destruction of the Temple in Jerusalem in 70 CE the lamb was omitted, but the meal continued and other foods added, as well as the four cups of wine, each one given a symbolic meaning. However, food was not the primary purpose of the celebration. It was to help each generation experience the foundational event of Jewish history and to understand its implications for Jews in every generation; and above all, to teach the children about the Exodus. This is already emphasised in the Torah: 'You shall tell your child (*v'higgad'ta l'vin'cha*) on

that day…' (Exodus 13:8). This telling and celebration became known as *Seder Haggadah*, the 'Order of Narration'. In time, it became customary for Ashkenazi Jews to use the term *Seder* for the celebration and rituals of the first eve of *Pesach* and *Haggadah* for the book containing the text of the celebration.

The *Haggadah*

As with all Jewish liturgy, the initial transmission of the 'text' of the *Haggadah* was oral, gradually becoming fixed around the 9th century CE. In the ensuing period countless manuscript editions were produced, some richly illustrated and belonging to the masterpieces of Jewish religious art. Since the invention of printing, several thousand different *Haggadot* have been published, with an increasing number each year (nowadays appearing on the internet, as well as in hard copy). Although they maintain essentially the same structure, there are many variations, based on local custom, differences of theological emphasis or the social environment in which they were produced. Of the making of *Haggadot* there is no end!

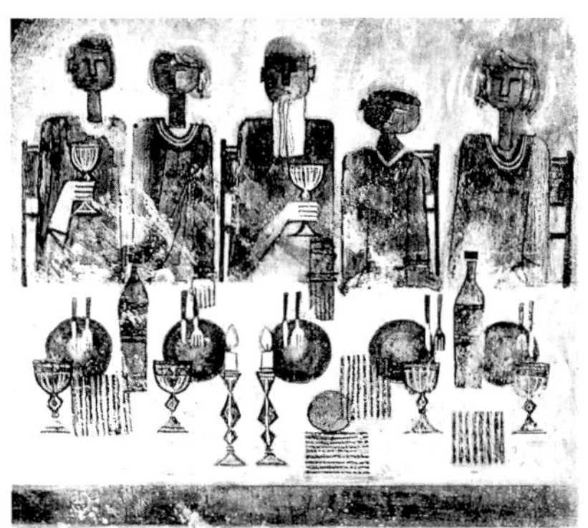

Jacob Shacham – ULPS Haggadah 1968

This *Haggadah*

This is the fourth *Haggadah* produced by the Liberal Jewish movement in Britain, and the first to include full transliteration.

A much shortened text appeared in 1918 with an amplified version produced in 1962 (republished with illustrations by Jacob Shacham in 1968). A third *Haggadah* appeared in 1981 with a fuller, more traditional text although with minor alterations to the order of passages to facilitate a more logical sequence of themes. It was the work of Rabbi John D Rayner (in collaboration with Rabbi Chaim Stern and Rabbi Julia Neuberger). Illustrations were chosen from a variety of medieval *Haggadot* by Nurit Beeri and Rabbi Lawrence Rigal. The English was modernised: no more 'thees' and 'thous' in line with the then current ULPS prayerbooks. A further modernisation of the English text by Rabbi Jonathan Keren Black appeared in 1990. In line with the current Liberal Jewish liturgy, it introduced gender-neutral language, neither God nor humans being addressed in male terminology, with 'king' becoming 'ruler' and 'Lord' becoming 'Eternal One'.

The rabbi checks the flour before the matzah dough is prepared
New York, 1858

This *Haggadah* largely follows the 1981 Hebrew text of Rabbi Rayner and the English of Rabbi Keren Black. However, it does attempt to answer two conflicting needs that have become apparent to the editors in recent times: the need to include innovative readings and yet the desire by many to shorten the time spent on the basic text of the *Seder*. Therefore, for the first half of the *Seder*, (i.e. up to the meal on page 21a) the essential text of the *Haggadah* is printed on the right-hand pages (with suffix 'a'), with the facing page (suffix 'b') containing additional material: explanations, songs and reflective passages. The leader of the *Seder* can choose to read only the right-hand pages, or include material from the left-hand pages to suit the wishes of the gathering. The pages of the second half of the *Seder* are numbered sequentially, though some elements can be omitted at the discretion of the leader.

As an alternative, a child-friendly *Seder* can be conducted by using this book from the English-opening end and working towards the centre. This short *Seder* could be augmented with sections from the main text as deemed appropriate (page references are incorporated to assist with this). Full details of this family-oriented version of the *Seder* and guidance for its use can be found at the other end of the book.

Illustrations

We have chosen illustrations from a selection of *Haggadot* to show the variety of settings in which the *Seder* has been celebrated historically. The sources of these illustrations and full notes on the origins of the written text can be found on the following website address: **www.liberaljudaism.org/haggadah**. In time this website will also include additional material to supplement the 'b' pages of this *Haggadah*. The website will also carry guidelines regarding preparations for *Pesach*, the setting up of the *Seder* table and suggestions of how to lead the *Seder*.

We hope that this *Haggadah* will inspire a new generation of Jews to enliven their *Seder*, be it held at home or communally, and that it will enable a wide range of *Sedarim* to be easily conducted from the same book.

Rabbi Dr Andrew Goldstein and Rabbi Pete Tobias
January 2010/*Sh'vat 5770*

Haggadah B'chol Dor Va-Dor

A Haggadah for all Generations

Opening prayer

Long ago, at this season, on a night such as this, a people – our people – set out on a journey.

All but crushed by their enslavement, they yet recalled the far-off memory of a happier past,

And heard the voice of their ancestral God, bidding them summon up the courage to be free.

Bravely, they went forth from Egypt, crossed the sea, and headed through the desert for the Promised Land.

What they experienced, they remembered, and told their children, and they to theirs.

From generation to generation, the story was retold, and we are here to tell it yet again.

We too give thanks for Israel's liberation; we too remember what it means to be a slave.

And so we pray for all who are still fettered, still denied their human rights.

Let all God's children sit at the table of the Eternal One, drink the wine of deliverance, eat the bread of freedom:

freedom from bondage — *and freedom from oppression*

freedom from hunger — *and freedom from want*

freedom from hatred — *and freedom from fear*

freedom to think — *and freedom to speak*

freedom to learn — *and freedom to love*

freedom to hope — *and freedom to rejoice*

soon, in our days. — *Amen.*

(John D Rayner)

Seder checklist

The following order of the *Seder*, slightly different from the traditional version, is offered as a guide to set out the various stages of the *Seder* that follows. It is intended to be recited as a rhyme and also serves as a 'checklist' for the elements that should be included.

Neirot	Lighting the Candles	נֵרוֹת
Kaddeish	Making *Kiddush*	קַדֵּשׁ
Karpas	Green herbs	כַּרְפַּס
Lachma	Bread of Affliction	לַחְמָא
Arba'ah	Four Questions, Four Children	אַרְבָּעָה
Haggadah	Telling the Story	הַגָּדָה
Pesach	*Pesach* – Passover sacrifice	פֶּסַח
Matzah	*Matzah* – Unleavened Bread	מַצָּה
Maror	*Maror* – Bitter Herbs	מָרוֹר
Koreich	The Hillel Sandwich	כּוֹרֵךְ
Shulchan Oreich	The Meal	שֻׁלְחָן עוֹרֵךְ
Tzafun	The *Afikoman*	צָפוּן
Bareich	Thanksgiving for the Meal	בָּרֵךְ
Hallel	Praise	הַלֵּל
Nirtzah	Conclusion	נִרְצָה

Michel Kichka

Neirot נֵרוֹת

Lighting the candles

We praise You, Eternal God, Sovereign of the universe: You sanctify us by Your commandments and enjoin us to kindle the (Sabbath and) festival lights.

בָּרוּךְ אַתָּה יְיָ אֱלֹהֵינוּ מֶלֶךְ הָעוֹלָם, אֲשֶׁר קִדְּשָׁנוּ בְּמִצְוֹתָיו, וְצִוָּנוּ לְהַדְלִיק נֵר שֶׁל (שַׁבָּת וְשֶׁל) יוֹם טוֹב.

Baruch atah Adonai eloheinu melech ha-olam, asher kidd'shanu b'mitzvotav v'tzivvanu l'hadlik neir shel (shabbat v'shel) yom tov.

Shabbat Candles – Marc Chagall

A blessing for all who are gathered to celebrate the *Seder.*

May God bless you and keep you.
May God look kindly upon you and be gracious to you. May God reach out to you in tenderness and give you peace.

יְבָרֶכְךָ יְהוָֹה וְיִשְׁמְרֶךָ.
יָאֵר יְהוָֹה פָּנָיו אֵלֶיךָ וִיחֻנֶּךָּ.
יִשָּׂא יְהוָֹה פָּנָיו אֵלֶיךָ וְיָשֵׂם לְךָ שָׁלוֹם.

Y'varech'cha Adonai v'yishm'recha.
Ya'eir Adonai panav eilecha viychunneka.
Yissa Adonai panav eilecha v'yaseim l'cha shalom.

Opening prayers

Sharing *Seder* with Family

We thank You, O God, for our family and for what we mean and bring to one another. We are grateful for the bonds of loyalty and affection which sustain us and which keep us close to one another no matter how far apart we may be.

We thank You for implanting within us the capacity to love and to care.

Help us to be modest in our demands of one another, but generous in our giving to each other. May we never measure how much love or encouragement we offer; or count the number of times we forgive. Rather, may we always be grateful that we have one another and that we are able to express our love in acts of kindness.

Bless our family with health, happiness, and contentment. Above all, grant us the wisdom to build a joyous and peaceful home in which Your spirit will always abide.

Sharing *Seder* with Friends and/or Community

We are grateful, O God, for the inspiration and joy of this Festival of *Pesach* and for the companionship of those who sit around this table on this sacred night. May this *Seder* strengthen the bond of friendship amongst us and help us to value the support we give each other. May our celebrations deepen our commitment to the Jewish heritage and encourage us to seek the wellbeing of our people wherever they may live. May the story we now tell inspire us to seek the freedom of all who are enslaved, of all who live in darkness and oppression.

Berlin, 1927

Kaddeish קַדֵּשׁ

The glasses are filled

The first glass כּוֹס שֶׁל קִדּוּשׁ

We raise our glasses in acknowledgement of the first of God's promises:

Say to the Israelite people: 'I am the Eternal One and **I will release you** from Egyptian oppression.' (Exodus 6:6)

אֱמֹר לִבְנֵי־יִשְׂרָאֵל: "אֲנִי יְהוָה **וְהוֹצֵאתִי** אֶתְכֶם מִתַּחַת סִבְלֹת מִצְרַיִם."

We praise You, Eternal God, Sovereign of the universe, Creator of the fruit of the vine.

בָּרוּךְ אַתָּה יְיָ אֱלֹהֵינוּ מֶלֶךְ הָעוֹלָם, בּוֹרֵא פְּרִי הַגָּפֶן.

Baruch atah Adonai eloheinu melech ha-olam borei p'ri ha-gafen.

We praise You, Eternal God, Sovereign of the universe. You have called us from all peoples that we might serve You, and taught us laws to sanctify our lives. In Your love You have given us (Sabbath days for rest and) festive days and seasons for rejoicing. We thank You for this (Sabbath and this) Festival of Unleavened Bread, our Season of Freedom that we may join in worship and remember the Exodus from Egypt. For You have called us to serve You as a holy people, and given us (the Sabbath, a token of Your love and favour, and) festivals for gladness and joy. We praise You, O God: You sanctify (the Sabbath,) the House of Israel and the festive seasons.

בָּרוּךְ אַתָּה יְיָ אֱלֹהֵינוּ מֶלֶךְ הָעוֹלָם, אֲשֶׁר בָּחַר בָּנוּ מִכׇּל־עָם וְקֵרְבָנוּ לַעֲבוֹדָתוֹ וְקִדְּשָׁנוּ בְּמִצְוֹתָיו וַתִּתֶּן־לָנוּ, יְיָ אֱלֹהֵינוּ, בְּאַהֲבָה (שַׁבָּתוֹת לִמְנוּחָה וּ) מוֹעֲדִים לְשִׂמְחָה, חַגִּים וּזְמַנִּים לְשָׂשׂוֹן. אֶת־יוֹם (הַשַּׁבָּת הַזֶּה וְאֶת־יוֹם) חַג הַמַּצּוֹת הַזֶּה, זְמַן חֵרוּתֵנוּ, מִקְרָא קֹדֶשׁ, זֵכֶר לִיצִיאַת מִצְרָיִם, כִּי בָנוּ בָחַרְתָּ וְאוֹתָנוּ קֵרַבְתָּ לַעֲבוֹדָתֶךָ (וְשַׁבָּת) וּמוֹעֲדֵי קָדְשְׁךָ (בְּאַהֲבָה וּבְרָצוֹן) בְּשִׂמְחָה וּבְשָׂשׂוֹן הִנְחַלְתָּנוּ. בָּרוּךְ אַתָּה יְיָ, מְקַדֵּשׁ (הַשַּׁבָּת וְ) יִשְׂרָאֵל וְהַזְּמַנִּים.

Baruch atah Adonai eloheinu melech ha-olam asher bachar banu mi-kol am v'keirvanu la'avodato, v'kidd'shanu b'mitzvotav, va-tittein lanu, Adonai eloheinu, b'ahavah (Shabbatot lim'nuchah, u-) mo'adim l'simchah, chaggim u-z'manim l'sason. Et yom (ha-Shabbat ha-zeh v'et yom) chag ha-matzot ha-zeh, z'man cheiruteinu, mikra kodesh, zeicher liytziy'at mitzrayim. Ki vanu vacharta v'otanu keiravta la-avodatecha (v'Shabbat) u-mo'adei kodsh'cha (b'ahavah u-v'ratzon) b'simchah u-v'sason hinchaltanu. Baruch atah Adonai, m'kaddeish (ha-Shabbat v') yisra'el v'ha-z'mannim.

Before drinking, we say *She-hecheyanu* at the foot of page 4a.
On a Saturday night, this is preceded by *Havdalah*.

Why do we drink four glasses of wine?

New York, 1921

There are many ways of interpreting the four glasses of wine. Some say they represent the 'four corners of the earth', for freedom must reign everywhere, the four seasons of the year, for freedom must be guarded at all times, the 'four empires' (Egypt, Babylon, Greece and Rome) that oppressed the Jews in days of old, for all tyranny must pass away before all the world is free.

Above all, they represent the four promises of redemption in the biblical account of the escape from Egypt:

Say to the Israelite people: 'I am the Eternal One and **I will release you** from Egyptian oppression and **I will deliver you** from serving them. **I will redeem you** with an outstretched arm and with great acts of judgement and **I will take you** to be My people and I will be your God; that you might know that I am the Eternal One, your God, who will bring you out from Egyptian oppression.'
(Exodus 6:6-7)

אֱמֹר לִבְנֵי־יִשְׂרָאֵל אֲנִי יְהוָֹה **וְהוֹצֵאתִי** אֶתְכֶם מִתַּחַת סִבְלֹת מִצְרַיִם **וְהִצַּלְתִּי** אֶתְכֶם מֵעֲבֹדָתָם **וְגָאַלְתִּי** אֶתְכֶם בִּזְרוֹעַ נְטוּיָה וּבִשְׁפָטִים גְּדֹלִים. **וְלָקַחְתִּי** אֶתְכֶם לִי לְעָם וְהָיִיתִי לָכֶם לֵאלֹהִים וִידַעְתֶּם כִּי אֲנִי יְהוָֹה אֱלֹהֵיכֶם הַמּוֹצִיא אֶתְכֶם מִתַּחַת סִבְלוֹת מִצְרָיִם.

On Saturday night, continue with *Havdalah*,
looking at the festival candles while reading the following:

We praise You, Eternal God, Sovereign of the universe, Creator of the lights of fire. We praise You, Eternal God, Sovereign of the universe, for You have taught us to distinguish between holy and mundane, light and darkness, between the seventh day and the six days of work, between the holiness of the Sabbath and the holiness of the festivals. We praise You O God, for teaching us to distinguish between holy and holy.

בָּרוּךְ אַתָּה יְיָ, אֱלֹהֵינוּ מֶלֶךְ הָעוֹלָם, בּוֹרֵא מְאוֹרֵי הָאֵשׁ.
בָּרוּךְ אַתָּה יְיָ, אֱלֹהֵינוּ מֶלֶךְ הָעוֹלָם, הַמַּבְדִּיל בֵּין קֹדֶשׁ לְחֹל, בֵּין אוֹר לְחֹשֶׁךְ, בֵּין יוֹם הַשְּׁבִיעִי לְשֵׁשֶׁת יְמֵי הַמַּעֲשֶׂה, בֵּין קְדֻשַּׁת הַשַּׁבָּת לִקְדֻשַּׁת יוֹם טוֹב.
בָּרוּךְ אַתָּה יְיָ, הַמַּבְדִּיל בֵּין קֹדֶשׁ לְקֹדֶשׁ.

Baruch atah Adonai eloheinu melech ha-olam borei m'orei ha-eish.
Baruch atah Adonai eloheinu melech ha-olam ha-mavdil bein kodesh l'chol, bein or l'choshech, bein yom ha-sh'vi'i l'sheishet y'mei ha-ma'aseh, bein k'dushat shabbat likdushat yom tov hivdalta.
Baruch atah Adonai ha-mavdil bein kodesh l'kodesh.

New York, 1929

We thank God for enabling us to share *Seder* by reciting together:

We praise You, Eternal God, Sovereign of the universe, that You have kept us alive, sustained us, and enabled us to reach this season.

בָּרוּךְ אַתָּה יְיָ אֱלֹהֵינוּ מֶלֶךְ הָעוֹלָם, שֶׁהֶחֱיָנוּ וְקִיְּמָנוּ וְהִגִּיעָנוּ לַזְּמַן הַזֶּה.

Baruch atah Adonai eloheinu melech ha-olam she-hecheyanu v'kiyy'manu v'higgiy'anu la-z'man ha-zeh.

Lean to the left and drink the first glass of wine

Water at the *Seder*: the role of Miriam

There is a tradition that, prior to the *Karpas* (green herb) the hands are washed without saying a blessing. Water plays a prominent part in the story of the Exodus and, on each occasion, Miriam is involved. (This theme will be followed at various stages of our *Haggadah*.) The story of redemption begins when Moses is saved from the River Nile while Miriam watches over him:

Haggdah l'leyl shimmurim, Frankfurt am Main 1926

When Moses' mother could hide him no longer, she got a papyrus basket for him and coated it with tar and pitch. Then she placed the child in it and put it among the reeds along the bank of the Nile. His sister stood at a distance to see what would happen to him. Then Pharaoh's daughter went down to the Nile to bathe, and her attendants were walking along the river bank. She saw the basket among the reeds and sent her slave girl to get it. (Exodus 2:3-5)

וְלֹא־יָכְלָה עוֹד הַצְּפִינוֹ וַתִּקַּח־לוֹ תֵּבַת גֹּמֶא וַתַּחְמְרָה בַחֵמָר וּבַזָּפֶת וַתָּשֶׂם בָּהּ אֶת־הַיֶּלֶד וַתָּשֶׂם בַּסּוּף עַל־שְׂפַת הַיְאֹר. וַתֵּתַצַּב אֲחֹתוֹ מֵרָחֹק לְדֵעָה מַה־יֵּעָשֶׂה לוֹ. וַתֵּרֶד בַּת־פַּרְעֹה לִרְחֹץ עַל־הַיְאֹר וְנַעֲרֹתֶיהָ הֹלְכֹת עַל־יַד הַיְאֹר וַתֵּרֶא אֶת־הַתֵּבָה בְּתוֹךְ הַסּוּף וַתִּשְׁלַח אֶת־אֲמָתָהּ וַתִּקָּחֶהָ.

כִּי הֶעֱלִתִיךָ מֵאֶרֶץ מִצְרַיִם וּמִבֵּית עֲבָדִים פְּדִיתִיךָ
וָאֶשְׁלַח לְפָנֶיךָ אֶת־מֹשֶׁה אַהֲרֹן וּמִרְיָם.

I brought you up out of Egypt and redeemed you from the land of slavery.
I sent Moses, Aaron and Miriam to lead you. (Micah 6:4)

Karpas כַּרְפַּס

Green Herbs

When earth is freed
from winter's yoke,
when lambs are born
and trees turn green,
then we recall our liberation
from Egypt's bondage
one such springtime, long ago.
For us too may this be
a season of renewal
of life and growth,
of hope and love.
(John D Rayner)

Paul Solomons 2010

Rise up my love,
my fair one, come away!
For lo the winter is past,
the rain is over and gone,
the flowers appear on the earth,
the time of singing has come,
and the song of the dove
is heard in our land.
(Song of Songs 2:10-12)

קוּמִי לָךְ רַעְיָתִי יָפָתִי וּלְכִי־לָךְ.
כִּי־הִנֵּה הַסְּתָיו עָבָר
הַגֶּשֶׁם חָלַף הָלַךְ לוֹ.
הַנִּצָּנִים נִרְאוּ בָאָרֶץ
עֵת הַזָּמִיר הִגִּיעַ
וְקוֹל הַתּוֹר נִשְׁמַע בְּאַרְצֵנוּ.

Kumi lach ra'yati yafati u-l'chi lach. Ki hinneih ha-stav avar ha-geshem chalaf halach lo. Ha-nitzanim nir'u va-aretz eit ha-zamir higgi'a v'kol ha-tor nishma b'artzeinu.

We praise You, Eternal God, Sovereign of the universe, Creator of the fruit of the earth.

בָּרוּךְ אַתָּה יְיָ אֱלֹהֵינוּ מֶלֶךְ הָעוֹלָם, בּוֹרֵא פְּרִי הָאֲדָמָה.

Baruch atah Adonai eloheinu melech ha-olam borei p'ri ha-adamah.

The *Karpas* is dipped in salt water and eaten

How astonishing… is the growth of foods from seeds. A single grain that has been saved from mishaps produces a thousand grains and more. It has even been said that out of one grain of wheat, as many as three hundred (stalks) will spring up, each containing over twenty grains. We also come across gigantic trees whose roots have sprung out of a single seed or a single shoot… Praised be the All-Wise and Gracious One who brings into existence such vast effects from causes so small and weak.
Bachya ben Joseph ibn Pakuda (c.1050-1120)

Four explanations for the *Karpas* and dipping in salt water:
1. It is springtime, therefore we acknowledge that the world is turning green after winter.
2. The *Seder* emulates a Roman banquet and *Karpas* is intended as an hors-d'oeuvres.
3. It reminds us of the hyssop that was dipped in the lamb's blood which was painted on the doorposts of the Hebrews in Egypt at the time of the Exodus (Exodus 12:22).
4. As with other elements of the *Seder*, it arouses children's curiosity, reminding them of the salty water of the Sea of Reeds or the sweat and tears of the Hebrew slaves.

The Song of Songs is traditionally recited at *Pesach* because of its references to Spring

♪ דּוֹדִי לִי

דּוֹדִי לִי וַאֲנִי לוֹ הָרֹעֶה בַּשּׁוֹשַׁנִּים.
מִי זֹאת עֹלָה מִן־הַמִּדְבָּר
מִי זֹאת עֹלָה
מְקֻטֶּרֶת מוֹר וּלְבוֹנָה?
לִבַּבְתִּנִי אֲחֹתִי כַלָּה
לִבַּבְתִּינִי כַלָּה.
עוּרִי צָפוֹן וּבוֹאִי תֵימָן.

Dodi li

My beloved is mine and I am his
who pastures among the lilies.
Who is that coming out of the desert,
perfumed with myrrh and incense?
Who is it?
You have taken my heart, my sister,
my bride, you have taken my heart.
Rise up O North wind,
and come, O South wind.
(Song of Songs 2:16; 3:6; 4:9, 16)

Dodi li va-ani lo ha-ro'eh ba-shoshannim.
Mi zot olah min ha-midbar, mi zot olah?
M'kutteret mor, mor u-l'vonah.
Libbavtini achoti challah, libbavtini challah
Uri tzafon u-vo'i teiman, uri tzafon u-vo'i teiman.

Lachma לַחְמָא

Bread of Affliction

The leader takes the middle *Matzah* and breaks it in two. The larger piece is the *Afikoman*, which will be hidden away; the smaller piece is replaced between the two whole *Matzot*, which are lifted as the following is recited.

This is the bread of affliction our ancestors ate in the land of Egypt.

Let all who are hungry come and eat; Let all who are in need come and share our Passover.

This year here, next year in the land of Israel;

This year oppressed, next year free.

הָא לַחְמָא עַנְיָא דִי אֲכַלוּ
אַבְהָתַנָא בְּאַרְעָא דְמִצְרָיִם.
כָּל־דִּכְפִין יֵיתֵי וְיֵכֻל,
כָּל־דִּצְרִיךְ יֵיתֵי וְיִפְסַח.
הָשַׁתָּא הָכָא,
לְשַׁתָּא דְאַתְיָא בְּאַרְעָא דְיִשְׂרָאֵל.
הָשַׁתָּא עַבְדֵי,
לְשַׁתָּא דְאַתְיָא בְּנֵי חוֹרִין.

Ha lachma anya di achalu avhatana b'ar'a d'mitzrayim.
Kol dichfin yeitei v'yeichul
Kol ditzrich yeitei v'yif'sach.
Ha-shata hacha – l'shata d'atya b'ar'a d'yisra'el
Ha-shata avdei – l'shata d'atya b'nei chorin.

Mark Weinberg, American Hebrew, April 1908

'This year here, next year in the land of Israel…' 'Here' is wherever any human beings are still enslaved, or deprived of their rights; 'the Land of Israel' is the symbol of the hope of redemption. The journey of our ancestors is the journey of every people, and of every generation, until the Promised Land is reached by all, and freedom becomes the heritage of all God's children. (John D Rayner)

Slavery

A question to ask before the traditional four questions: Why is this night no different from all other nights? Because on this night, millions of human beings around the world are still enslaved, or deprived of their rights, just as they are on all other nights. As we celebrate our freedom tonight, we remember them.

The children and adults who work in sweatshops of the developing world to produce the cheap clothes wealthier consumers are eager to buy.

The adults or children sold into a lifetime of slavery to pay a debt, or those captured in war by slave traders, even in the modern world.

The women and men from Eastern Europe and elsewhere traded into a life of degradation as sex slaves in the West.

The men, women and children forced to live in abject poverty by the lack of care by many nations' leaders and insensitive citizens.

May the message of this Festival of *Pesach* be clear to us and all the world: we cannot celebrate it properly unless we commit ourselves to working for the liberty of all who are enslaved. The symbols on the *Seder* table, the unleavened bread we shall eat for the next seven days, are to remind us that there is still oppression in our world and that we are obliged to work to remove it from society.

Breaking the *Matzah*: traditionally the larger piece is put away for the *Afikoman*. Once Menachem of Lubavitch observed a guest carefully measuring the two pieces. The rebbe remarked, 'When greatness has to be measured in millimetres, it is not greatness at all. In such instances the lesser may be greater.' At the *Seder* we are all equal, the poor and the rich, the powerful and the weak: all are God's children. The *Seder* should remind us that we are all equal in God's eyes and therefore we should treat all human beings with respect.

Arba'ah אַרְבָּעָה

The four questions

It is traditional for the youngest person present to ask these four questions:

How different is this night from all other nights!

מַה נִּשְׁתַּנָּה הַלַּיְלָה הַזֶּה מִכָּל הַלֵּילוֹת!

On all other nights we eat either leavened or unleavened bread; why only unleavened bread tonight?

שֶׁבְּכָל הַלֵּילוֹת אָנוּ אוֹכְלִין חָמֵץ וּמַצָּה,
הַלַּיְלָה הַזֶּה כֻּלּוֹ מַצָּה?

On all other nights we eat different types of herbs and vegetables; why bitter herbs tonight?

שֶׁבְּכָל הַלֵּילוֹת אָנוּ אוֹכְלִין שְׁאָר יְרָקוֹת,
הַלַּיְלָה הַזֶּה מָרוֹר?

On all other nights we do not even dip once; why do we dip twice tonight?

שֶׁבְּכָל הַלֵּילוֹת אֵין אָנוּ מַטְבִּילִין אֲפִילוּ
פַּעַם אֶחָת, הַלַּיְלָה הַזֶּה שְׁתֵּי פְעָמִים?

On all other nights we eat either sitting or leaning; why do we all lean tonight?

שֶׁבְּכָל הַלֵּילוֹת אָנוּ אוֹכְלִין בֵּין יוֹשְׁבִין
וּבֵין מְסֻבִּין, הַלַּיְלָה הַזֶּה כֻּלָּנוּ מְסֻבִּין?

Mah nishtanah ha-lailah ha-zeh mi-kol ha-leilot!

She-b'chol ha-leilot anu ochlin chameitz u-matzah,
ha-lailah ha-zeh kullo matzah?

She-b'chol ha-leilot anu ochlin sh'ar y'rakot,
ha-lailah ha-zeh maror?

She-b'chol ha-leilot ein anu matbilin
afilu pa'am echat, ha-lailah ha-zeh sh'tei f'amim?

She-b'chol ha-leilot anu ochlin
bein yoshvin u-vein m'subin,
ha-lailah ha-zeh kullanu m'subin?

Paul Solomons, 2010

The glasses are filled

The role of children in the *Seder*

The celebration of the *Seder* has been designed especially for teaching children, as it is written: 'and you shall tell your child on that day… and when your children ask you, you shall tell them…' (Exodus 13: 8, 14)

Rabbi Yehudah says that parched grain and nuts should be given to children on *erev Pesach* to encourage them to stay awake and ask questions about the *Seder.*

You are free to ask, you are free to question,
free to learn the answers of tradition,
free to add answers of your own!
(Rabbi Chaim Stern)

The four questions have been a feature of the *Seder* for so many generations and in so many places. In recognition of this, here are the same questions in Ladino and in Yiddish:

Ladino

Kuanto fue mud'ad'a la noce la esta, mas ke tod'as las noces.

Ke en tod'as las noces nos komientes levdo o sesenia, i la noce la esta tod'o el sesenia.

Ke en tod'as las noces nos komientes resto de ved'ruras, i la noce la esta licuga.

Ke en tod'as las noces, non nos entinientes afilu ves una, i la noce la esta dos vezes.

Ke en tod'as las noces nos komientes i beviente, tanto asentad'os tanto areskovdad'os, i la noce la esta tod'os nos areskovdad'os.

Yiddish

Tate, Ich vil dir fregen di fier kashes:

Vee azoi iz di nacht fun Pesach anders fun alle necht fun a gantz yor?

In alle necht fun a gantz yor, esn mir chometz un matzo. Ober di nacht fun Pesach esn mir nor matzo.

In alle necht fun a gantz yor, esn mir alerley grinsn. Ober di nacht fun Pesach esn mir nor bitere grinsn.

In alle necht fun a gantz yor, tunken mir nit ayn, afilu eyn mol nit. Ober di nacht fun Pesach, tunken mir ayn, tsvey mol – eyn mol chreyn in charoyses, un dos tsveyte mol a tsibele in salts-vaser

In alle necht fun a gantz yor, esn mir say zitsindik un say ongelent. Ober di nacht fun Pesach, esn mir alle ongelent.

The *Matzah* is uncovered for the narration

A response to the four questions: our story begins…

We were slaves to Pharaoh in Egypt, and the Eternal One our God led us out from there with a mighty hand and an outstretched arm. If the Holy One, ever to be praised, had not led our ancestors out of Egypt, we and our children and children's children would have remained slaves to Pharaoh in Egypt. Therefore, even if we were all wise and discerning, all scholars and experts in Torah, it would still be our duty to retell the story of the Exodus; and those who linger over the telling are worthy of praise.

עֲבָדִים הָיִינוּ לְפַרְעֹה בְּמִצְרָיִם, וַיּוֹצִיאֵנוּ יְיָ אֱלֹהֵינוּ מִשָּׁם בְּיָד חֲזָקָה וּבִזְרוֹעַ נְטוּיָה. וְאִלּוּ לֹא הוֹצִיא הַקָּדוֹשׁ בָּרוּךְ הוּא אֶת־אֲבֹתֵינוּ מִמִּצְרָיִם, הֲרֵי אָנוּ וּבָנֵינוּ וּבְנֵי בָנֵינוּ מְשֻׁעְבָּדִים הָיִינוּ לְפַרְעֹה בְּמִצְרָיִם. וַאֲפִילוּ כֻּלָּנוּ חֲכָמִים, כֻּלָּנוּ נְבוֹנִים, כֻּלָּנוּ זְקֵנִים, כֻּלָּנוּ יוֹדְעִים אֶת־הַתּוֹרָה, מִצְוָה עָלֵינוּ לְסַפֵּר בִּיצִיאַת מִצְרָיִם, וְכָל־הַמַּרְבֶּה לְסַפֵּר בִּיצִיאַת מִצְרָיִם הֲרֵי זֶה מְשֻׁבָּח.

Avadim hayinu l'far'oh b'mitzrayim va-yotzi'einu Adonai eloheinu mi-sham b'yad chazakah u-vizro'a n'tuyah. V'illu lo hotzi ha-kadosh baruch hu et avoteinu mi-mitzrayim, harei anu u-vaneinu u-v'nei vaneinu m'shubbadim hayinu l'far'oh b'mitzrayim. V'afilu kullanu chachamim, kullanu n'vonim, kullanu z'keinim, kullanu yod'im et ha-Torah, mitzvah aleinu l'sapeir b'tziy'at mitzrayim, v'chol ha-marbeh l'sapeir b'tziy'at mitzrayim harei zeh m'shubbach.

Siegmund Forst, New York, 1959

There is a story about Rabbi Eliezer, Rabbi Joshua, Rabbi Eleazar son of Azariah, Rabbi Akiva and Rabbi Tarfon. They once held a *Seder* at B'nei B'rak. They went on talking about the Exodus from Egypt all that night, until finally their pupils came and said to them: 'Masters, it is now time to recite the morning *Sh'ma!*'

מַעֲשֶׂה בְּרַבִּי אֱלִיעֶזֶר וְרַבִּי יְהוֹשֻׁעַ וְרַבִּי אֶלְעָזָר בֶּן עֲזַרְיָה וְרַבִּי עֲקִיבָא וְרַבִּי טַרְפוֹן שֶׁהָיוּ מְסֻבִּין בִּבְנֵי בְרַק, וְהָיוּ מְסַפְּרִים בִּיצִיאַת מִצְרַיִם כָּל־אוֹתוֹ הַלַּיְלָה עַד שֶׁבָּאוּ תַלְמִידֵיהֶם וְאָמְרוּ לָהֶם "רַבּוֹתֵינוּ, הִגִּיעַ זְמַן קְרִיאַת שְׁמַע שֶׁל שַׁחֲרִית!"

What were the five rabbis discussing all night? Some say they were debating the merits of the Bar Kochba rebellion against the Romans: to back open warfare or to encourage spiritual resistance. Rabbi Akiva favoured the former course of action, Rabbi Tarfon the latter. Another explanation speaks to many sitting down at *Seder* in every generation. Rabbi Eliezer had been excommunicated by the other rabbis for his stubbornness in insisting his view was valid, even though he was in a minority of one. The ban was lifted only as he lay dying… too late. Perhaps the *Seder* in B'nei Brak was just an idealised dream: when all the rabbis would sit at the same table. It tells us tonight all are welcome, even the Jews excluded by the family or who have excluded themselves. *Seder* night is a night for members of the family and a circle of friends to sit together, to forget the past slights and to remember values that really matter: freedom, tolerance and *sh'lom bayit* (family harmony).

Haggdah l'leyl shimmurim, Frankfurt am Main, 1926

Go down Moses

♪

When Israel was in Egypt's land – let my people go.
Oppressed so hard they could not stand – let my people go.

CHORUS *Go down, Moses, way down in Egypt's land*
Tell old Pharaoh, let my people go.

Thus saith the Lord bold Moses said – let my people go.
If not, I'll strike your firstborn dead – let my people go.

As Israel stood by the water's side – let my people go.
By God's command it did divide – let my people go.

No more shall they in bondage toil – let my people go.
Let them come out with Egypt's spoil – let my people go.

Arba'ah אַרְבָּעָה

The four children

כְּנֶגֶד אַרְבָּעָה בָנִים דִּבְּרָה תוֹרָה: אֶחָד חָכָם, וְאֶחָד רָשָׁע, וְאֶחָד תָּם וְאֶחָד שֶׁאֵינוֹ יוֹדֵעַ לִשְׁאוֹל.

The Torah alludes to four types of child: One who is wise, one who is wicked, one who is simple and one who does not know how to ask.

חָכָם מַה הוּא אוֹמֵר? מָה הָעֵדֹת וְהַחֻקִּים וְהַמִּשְׁפָּטִים אֲשֶׁר צִוָּה יְיָ אֱלֹהֵינוּ אֶתְכֶם? וְאַף אַתָּה אֱמָר־לוֹ כְּהִלְכוֹת הַפֶּסַח, אֵין מַפְטִירִין אַחַר הַפֶּסַח אֲפִיקוֹמָן.

What does the wise one say? 'What are the duties, laws and precepts which the Eternal God has commanded us?' To this child, teach all the laws of *Pesach*, even this difficult one, that 'one does not conclude the *Pesach* meal with *Afikoman*.'

רָשָׁע מַה הוּא אוֹמֵר? מָה הָעֲבוֹדָה הַזֹּאת לָכֶם? לָכֶם וְלֹא לוֹ. וּלְפִי שֶׁהוֹצִיא אֶת עַצְמוֹ מִן הַכְּלָל כָּפַר בָּעִקָּר. וְאַף אַתָּה הַקְהֵה אֶת שִׁנָּיו, וֶאֱמָר־לוֹ: בַּעֲבוּר זֶה עָשָׂה יְיָ לִי בְּצֵאתִי מִמִּצְרָיִם. לִי וְלֹא לוֹ. אִלּוּ הָיָה שָׁם לֹא הָיָה נִגְאָל.

What does the wicked one say? 'What is this service to you?' To you but not to me! If some should cut themselves off from our community and scorn our faith, make them eat their words, saying 'I do this because of what God did for me when I came out of Egypt.' For me but not for you! For had you been there, you would not have been redeemed.

תָּם מַה הוּא אוֹמֵר? מָה זֹּאת? וְאָמַרְתָּ אֵלָיו: בְּחוֹזֶק יָד הוֹצִיאָנוּ יְיָ מִמִּצְרָיִם, מִבֵּית עֲבָדִים.

What does the simple one say? 'What is this?' And you shall answer: 'With a mighty hand God led us out of Egypt, out of the house of bondage.'

וְשֶׁאֵינוֹ יוֹדֵעַ לִשְׁאוֹל, אַתְּ פְּתַח לוֹ, שֶׁנֶּאֱמַר: וְהִגַּדְתָּ לְבִנְךָ בַּיּוֹם הַהוּא בַּעֲבוּר זֶה עָשָׂה יְהוָֹה לִי בְּצֵאתִי מִמִּצְרָיִם.

And with the one who does not know how to ask, you must take the first step, as it is said: 'You shall tell your child on that day, "This is what God did for me when bringing me out of Egypt." '

The four children at the *Seder* table – which child am I?

As we celebrate this holiday of freedom, the ending of slavery, we ask 'Who am I when I hear of human rights abuses? Who will I choose to be when I know others are suffering?'
Will I be one who does not ask? Will I close the newspaper or turn off the television so that I do not hear? Will I turn my head and my heart away?
Will I ask only simple questions? 'What is this?' Will I ask 'what', but never 'why'?
Will I let the evil impulse, my *yetzer ha-ra*, **ask:** 'What has this to do with me?' Will I let the problem belong only to the victims or the do-gooders? Will I distance myself from those in need?
Or will I strive to act in wisdom, to ask: 'What are the underlying causes of the problem and what needs to be done to stop the abuse and free the oppressed? What are the laws and what does God expect of me?'

May God open the eyes of those who do not see, the mouths of those who do not ask, and the hearts of those who do not care, and grant us the wisdom to open our hands to our fellow humans when they are in need – the hand of generosity, the hand of support, the hand of peace and friendship.

♪ The ballad of the four children

Said the parents to the children:
'At the *Seder* you will dine;
You will eat your fill of *Matzah,*
You will drink four cups of wine.'

Now these parents had two daughters
With two sons they numbered four;
One was wise and one was wicked,
One was simple, filled with awe.

And the fourth was sweet and winsome,
He was young and he was small,
While the others asked the questions,
He could scarcely speak at all.

Said the wise one to the parents
'Would you please explain the laws
Of the customs of the *Seder*
Will you please explain the cause?'

And the parents proudly answered:
'Our ancestors ate in speed,
Ate the Paschal lamb 'ere midnight
And from slavery were freed.

'So we follow their example,
And by midnight must complete
All the *Seder,* and we should not
After twelve remain to eat.'

Then did sneer the one so wicked:
'What does all this mean to you?'
And the parents' voice was bitter
As their grief and anger grew.

'If yourself you don't consider
As a child of Israel
Then for you this has no meaning
You could be a slave as well.'

Then the simple one said simply,
'What is this?' and quietly,
The good parents told their offspring,
'We were freed from slavery.'

But the youngest one was silent
For he could not ask at all,
And his eyes were bright with wonder
As his parents told him all.

Now dear children, heed the lesson
And remember evermore,
What the parents told their children:
Sons and daughters numbered four.

A response to the four children: our story continues…

מִתְּחִלָּה עוֹבְדֵי עֲבוֹדָה זָרָה הָיוּ
אֲבוֹתֵינוּ, וְעַכְשָׁו קֵרְבָנוּ הַמָּקוֹם
לַעֲבוֹדָתוֹ, שֶׁנֶּאֱמַר: ״וַיֹּאמֶר יְהוֹשֻׁעַ
אֶל־כָּל־הָעָם כֹּה־אָמַר יְהֹוָה
אֱלֹהֵי יִשְׂרָאֵל בְּעֵבֶר הַנָּהָר יָשְׁבוּ
אֲבוֹתֵיכֶם מֵעוֹלָם תֶּרַח אֲבִי
אַבְרָהָם וַאֲבִי נָחוֹר וַיַּעַבְדוּ אֱלֹהִים
אֲחֵרִים. וָאֶקַּח אֶת־אֲבִיכֶם אֶת־
אַבְרָהָם מֵעֵבֶר הַנָּהָר וָאוֹלֵךְ אוֹתוֹ
בְּכָל־אֶרֶץ כְּנָעַן וָאַרְבֶּה אֶת־זַרְעוֹ
וָאֶתֶּן־לוֹ אֶת־יִצְחָק. וָאֶתֵּן לְיִצְחָק
אֶת־יַעֲקֹב וְאֶת־עֵשָׂו וָאֶתֵּן לְעֵשָׂו
אֶת־הַר שֵׂעִיר לָרֶשֶׁת אוֹתוֹ וְיַעֲקֹב
וּבָנָיו יָרְדוּ מִצְרָיִם.״

In the beginning our ancestors were idol worshippers, but now we have learnt to worship the true God, as it is said: 'Then Joshua spoke to all the people: Thus says the Eternal One, the God of Israel: Long ago in the days of Terach, the father of Abraham and Nachor, your ancestors lived beyond the River and worshipped other gods. Then I took your forefather Abraham from beyond the River and led him all over the land of Canaan. I blessed him with many descendants, for I gave him Isaac, and to Isaac I gave Jacob and Esau; and I let Esau take possession of Mount Se'ir. But Jacob and his children went down to Egypt.' (Joshua 24:2 ff.)

בָּרוּךְ שׁוֹמֵר הַבְטָחָתוֹ לְיִשְׂרָאֵל,
בָּרוּךְ הוּא.

Praised be the One whose promise to Israel never fails, praised be the Eternal.

Baruch shomeir havtachato l'yisra'el baruch hu.

The glasses are raised

וְהִיא שֶׁעָמְדָה לַאֲבוֹתֵינוּ וְלָנוּ,
שֶׁלֹּא אֶחָד בִּלְבַד עָמַד עָלֵינוּ
לְכַלּוֹתֵנוּ, אֶלָּא שֶׁבְּכָל־דּוֹר־וָדוֹר
עוֹמְדִים עָלֵינוּ לְכַלּוֹתֵנוּ, וְהַקָּדוֹשׁ
בָּרוּךְ הוּא מַצִּילֵנוּ מִיָּדָם.

God's promise has sustained our ancestors and it sustains us still. For not one enemy alone has sought to destroy us but in every generation enemies seek to destroy us, but the Eternal One, ever to be praised, delivers us from their power.

V'hi she-amdah la-avoteinu v'lanu she-lo echad bilvad amad aleinu l'challoteinu ella she-b'chol dor va-dor omdim aleinu l'challoteinu, v'ha-kadosh baruch hu matzileinu mi-yadam.

The glasses are lowered

Where does the story of the Jewish people begin?

The *Mishnah* (*Pesachim* 10:4) prescribes that the narrative of the *Haggadah* should 'begin with degradation and end with glory.' The *Gemara* (*Pesachim* 116a) asks 'what degradation?' – where is the real beginning of the story? Two great Babylonian sages of the 3rd century offer different answers. Shmuel, renowned for his practical expertise, sees it politically: 'We were slaves to Pharaoh in Egypt.' True degradation is physical slavery, true glory is liberation. Rav, the spiritual authority, places the beginning of the story earlier: 'In the beginning our ancestors were idol worshippers.' Real degradation is the spiritual darkness of idolatry, real freedom is found in the enlightenment of faith in one God. Jewish tradition, always respectful of different opinions, includes both these answers in the *Haggadah*.
(Rabbi Mark Solomon)

The Ethiopian Journey to the Land of Israel

The moon is watching from above
On my back is a light bag of food
The desert beneath me has no end ahead
And my mother promises my little brothers
'A little bit more, a little more
lift up your legs, a last push
towards Jerusalem.'

The moonlight stood fast
Our bag of food was lost.
The endless desert
Cries of jackals
And my mother comforts my little brothers
'A little bit more, a little more
soon we'll be redeemed
we won't stop going
to the Land of Israel.'

And at night bandits attacked
With a knife and sharp sword
In the desert, the blood of my mother
The moon is my witness and
I promise my brothers
'A little bit more, a little more
The dream will be fulfilled
One last effort before we get to Jerusalem.'

(Shlomo Gronich and the Sheba Choir.
Words by Chaim Idissis)

Siegmund Forst, 1955

Haggadah הַגָּדָה

Telling the story

אֲרַמִּי אֹבֵד אָבִי וַיֵּרֶד מִצְרַיְמָה וַיָּגָר
שָׁם בִּמְתֵי מְעָט וַיְהִי־שָׁם לְגוֹי גָּדוֹל
עָצוּם וָרָב. וַיָּרֵעוּ אֹתָנוּ הַמִּצְרִים
וַיְעַנּוּנוּ וַיִּתְּנוּ עָלֵינוּ עֲבֹדָה קָשָׁה.
וַנִּצְעַק אֶל־יְהוָֹה אֱלֹהֵי אֲבֹתֵינוּ
וַיִּשְׁמַע יְהוָֹה אֶת־קֹלֵנוּ וַיַּרְא
אֶת־עָנְיֵנוּ וְאֶת־עֲמָלֵנוּ וְאֶת־לַחֲצֵנוּ.
וַיּוֹצִאֵנוּ יְהוָֹה מִמִּצְרַיִם בְּיָד חֲזָקָה
וּבִזְרֹעַ נְטוּיָה וּבְמֹרָא גָּדֹל וּבְאֹתוֹת
וּבְמֹפְתִים.

Young Israel, Cincinnati, 1925

My father was a wandering Aramean, and he went down into Egypt with a few people and lived there and became a great nation, powerful and numerous. But the Egyptians mistreated us and made us suffer, putting us to hard labour. Then we cried out to the Eternal One, the God of our ancestors, and the Eternal One heard our voice and saw our misery, our toil and oppression. So the Eternal One brought us out of Egypt with a mighty hand and an outstretched arm, with great terror and with miraculous signs and wonders. (Deuteronomy 26:5-8)

Traditionally this passage, which contains the essential story of the Exodus from Egypt, forms the basis of a selection of rabbinic texts which comment on it. A selection of such texts follows; alternatively the story could be told through biblical texts, which start on the facing page.

Telling the story the rabbinic way – page 11a-13a

אֲרַמִּי אֹבֵד אָבִי.
לָמָּה נִקְרָא אֹבֵד? מְלַמֵּד שֶׁאָבְדוּ
אֲבוֹתֵינוּ בֵּין הָעַמִּים.

My father was a wandering Aramean. Why was he called a wanderer? This teaches that our ancestors wandered from place to place among the nations.

וַיֵּרֶד מִצְרַיְמָה.
מַשְׁמַע שֶׁלֹּא הָיְתָה יְרִידָה זוֹ מֵאֶרֶץ
כְּנַעַן לְאֶרֶץ מִצְרַיִם בִּלְבַד אֶלָּא אַף
יְרִידָה בְּרוּחַ, שֶׁהִשְׁתַּקְּעוּ בְּתוֹךְ
טֻמְאַת מִצְרַיִם.

And he went down to Egypt. *This shows that the descent was not only from Canaan to Egypt but that it was also a spiritual descent, for they became immersed in the corruption of Egypt.*

Continue on page 12a

Telling the story the biblical way – pages 11b-13b

The following verses have been extracted from the biblical version of the Exodus story. They may be read responsively.

There arose a new king over Egypt, who did not know Joseph. He said to his people, 'The Israelites have become too numerous for us. We must deal shrewdly with them or they will become even more numerous.'

וַיָּקָם מֶלֶךְ־חָדָשׁ עַל־מִצְרָיִם אֲשֶׁר
לֹא־יָדַע אֶת־יוֹסֵף. וַיֹּאמֶר אֶל־עַמּוֹ
הִנֵּה עַם בְּנֵי יִשְׂרָאֵל רַב וְעָצוּם מִמֶּנּוּ.
הָבָה נִתְחַכְּמָה לוֹ פֶּן־יִרְבֶּה.

So they put slave masters over them to oppress them with forced labour, and they built Pithom and Rameses as store cities for Pharaoh.

וַיָּשִׂימוּ עָלָיו שָׂרֵי מִסִּים לְמַעַן עַנֹּתוֹ
בְּסִבְלֹתָם וַיִּבֶן עָרֵי מִסְכְּנוֹת לְפַרְעֹה
אֶת־פִּתֹם וְאֶת־רַעַמְסֵס.

They made their lives bitter with hard labour in brick and mortar. The king of Egypt spoke to the Hebrew midwives, whose names were Shifrah and Pu'ah.

וַיְמָרְרוּ אֶת־חַיֵּיהֶם בַּעֲבֹדָה קָשָׁה
בְּחֹמֶר וּבִלְבֵנִים. וַיֹּאמֶר מֶלֶךְ מִצְרַיִם
לַמְיַלְּדֹת הָעִבְרִיֹּת אֲשֶׁר שֵׁם הָאַחַת
שִׁפְרָה וְשֵׁם הַשֵּׁנִית פּוּעָה.

Pharaoh said: 'When you help the Hebrew women in childbirth, if it is a boy, kill him.' The midwives, however, feared God and they let the boys live.

וַיֹּאמֶר בְּיַלֶּדְכֶן אֶת־הָעִבְרִיּוֹת וּרְאִיתֶן
אִם־בֵּן הוּא וַהֲמִתֶּן אֹתוֹ. וַתִּירֶאןָ
הַמְיַלְּדֹת אֶת־הָאֱלֹהִים וַתְּחַיֶּיןָ
אֶת־הַיְלָדִים.

Then Pharaoh gave this order to all his people: 'Every boy that is born you must throw into the Nile, but let every girl live.'

וַיְצַו פַּרְעֹה לְכָל־עַמּוֹ לֵאמֹר כָּל־הַבֵּן
הַיִּלּוֹד הַיְאֹרָה תַּשְׁלִיכֻהוּ וְכָל־הַבַּת
תְּחַיּוּן.

Now a man of the house of Levi married a Levite woman, and she became pregnant and gave birth to a son. When she saw that he was a fine child, she hid him for three months.

וַיֵּלֶךְ אִישׁ מִבֵּית לֵוִי וַיִּקַּח
אֶת־בַּת־לֵוִי. וַתַּהַר הָאִשָּׁה וַתֵּלֶד בֵּן
וַתֵּרֶא אֹתוֹ כִּי־טוֹב הוּא וַתִּצְפְּנֵהוּ
שְׁלֹשָׁה יְרָחִים.

Continue on page 12b

Telling the story the rabbinic way – 2

Continued from page 11a

And sojourned there with few numbers. As it is written, 'Your ancestors went down to Egypt, seventy persons in total.' You might have thought that they would assimilate among the Egyptians, but the verse continues 'and now the Eternal One your God has made you as numerous as the stars in the sky.' (Deut. 10:22)

וַיָּגָר שָׁם בִּמְתֵי מְעָט.
כְּמוֹ שֶׁנֶּאֱמַר: בְּשִׁבְעִים נֶפֶשׁ יָרְדוּ אֲבֹתֶיךָ מִצְרָיְמָה. יָכוֹל אָבְדוּ בֵּין הַמִּצְרִים? תַּלְמוּד לוֹמַר: וְעַתָּה שָׂמְךָ יְהֹוָה אֱלֹהֶיךָ כְּכוֹכְבֵי הַשָּׁמַיִם לָרֹב.

But there he became a great nation, mighty and numerous. *This teaches that the Israelites distinguished themselves in Egypt. They became unique through the mitzvot, until they were recognised and acknowledged as a separate nation. For they were not suspected of sexual immorality or of slander, nor did they change their names or their language.*

וַיְהִי־שָׁם לְגוֹי גָּדוֹל עָצוּם וָרָב.
מְלַמֵּד שֶׁהָיוּ יִשְׂרָאֵל מְצֻיָּנִים שָׁם. שֶׁהָיוּ מְסֻמָּנִים בְּמִצְוֹת עַד שֶׁהָיוּ יְדוּעִים וְנִכָּרִים כְּגוֹי בִּפְנֵי עַצְמוֹ. שֶׁלֹּא נֶחְשְׁדוּ עַל הָעֲרָיוֹת, וְלֹא עַל לְשׁוֹן הָרַע, וְלֹא שִׁנּוּ אֶת־שְׁמָם, וְלֹא שִׁנּוּ אֶת־לְשׁוֹנָם.

The Egyptians dealt harshly with us. They were ungrateful, for they paid back in evil the kindnesses that Joseph had done for them, as it is written, 'A new king arose over Egypt who knew not Joseph.' (Exodus 1:8). He pretended that he did not know Joseph.

וַיָּרֵעוּ אֹתָנוּ הַמִּצְרִים.
הָיוּ כְּפוּיֵי טוֹבָה, שֶׁשִּׁלְּמוּ רָעָה תַּחַת הַטּוֹבָה שֶׁעָשָׂה לָהֶם יוֹסֵף, כְּמוֹ שֶׁנֶּאֱמַר: וַיָּקָם מֶלֶךְ־חָדָשׁ עַל־מִצְרָיִם אֲשֶׁר לֹא־יָדַע אֶת־יוֹסֵף. עָשָׂה עַצְמוֹ כְּאִלּוּ לֹא יְדָעוֹ.

And they imposed hard labour on us. *The Egyptians would place a heavy burden on the weak, and a light burden on the strong; the burden of the old on the young, and the burden of the young on the old. This was work without end and done for no purpose, for the Egyptians wanted not only to enslave them but also to break their spirit.*

וַיִּתְּנוּ עָלֵינוּ עֲבֹדָה קָשָׁה.
שֶׁהָיוּ נוֹתְנִים מַשָּׂא גָּדוֹל עַל קָטָן וּמַשָּׂא קָטָן עַל גָּדוֹל, מַשָּׂא זָקֵן עַל בָּחוּר וּמַשָּׂא בָּחוּר עַל זָקֵן. הֲרֵי זוֹ עֲבוֹדָה שֶׁאֵין לָהּ קִצְבָה וְשֶׁנַּעֲשֵׂית לַשָּׁוְא. שֶׁלֹּא רָצוּ לְשַׁעְבֵּד אוֹתָם בִּלְבָד אֶלָּא אַף לִשְׁבֹּר רוּחָם.

Continue on page 13a

Telling the story the biblical way – 2

Continued from page 11b

But when she could hide him no longer, she got a papyrus basket for him. Placing the child in it, she put the basket among the reeds along the bank of the Nile. His sister stood at a distance to see what would happen to him.

וְלֹא־יָכְלָה עוֹד הַצְּפִינוֹ וַתִּקַּח־לוֹ תֵּבַת גֹּמֶא וַתַּחְמְרָה בַחֵמָר וּבַזָּפֶת
וַתָּשֶׂם בָּהּ אֶת־הַיֶּלֶד וַתָּשֶׂם בַּסּוּף עַל־שְׂפַת הַיְאֹר. וַתֵּתַצַּב אֲחֹתוֹ מֵרָחֹק לְדֵעָה מַה־יֵּעָשֶׂה לוֹ.

Then Pharaoh's daughter went down to the Nile to bathe. She saw the basket among the reeds and sent her slave girl to get it. 'This is one of the Hebrew babies,' she said.

וַתֵּרֶד בַּת־פַּרְעֹה לִרְחֹץ עַל־הַיְאֹר וַתֵּרֶא אֶת־הַתֵּבָה בְּתוֹךְ הַסּוּף וַתִּשְׁלַח אֶת־אֲמָתָהּ וַתִּקָּחֶהָ. וַתֹּאמֶר מִיַּלְדֵי הָעִבְרִים זֶה.

Then his sister asked Pharaoh's daughter, 'Shall I go and get one of the Hebrew women to nurse the baby for you?' 'Yes, go,' she answered. And the girl went and got the baby's mother.

וַתֹּאמֶר אֲחֹתוֹ אֶל־בַּת־פַּרְעֹה הַאֵלֵךְ וְקָרָאתִי לָךְ אִשָּׁה מֵינֶקֶת מִן הָעִבְרִיֹּת וְתֵינִק לָךְ אֶת־הַיָּלֶד וַתֹּאמֶר־לָהּ בַּת־פַּרְעֹה לֵכִי וַתֵּלֶךְ הָעַלְמָה וַתִּקְרָא אֶת־אֵם הַיָּלֶד.

When the child grew older, she took him to Pharaoh's daughter and he became her son. She named him Moses, saying, 'I drew him out of the water.'

וַיִּגְדַּל הַיֶּלֶד וַתְּבִאֵהוּ לְבַת־פַּרְעֹה וַיְהִי־לָהּ לְבֵן וַתִּקְרָא שְׁמוֹ מֹשֶׁה וַתֹּאמֶר כִּי מִן־הַמַּיִם מְשִׁיתִהוּ.

One day, after Moses had grown up, he went out to where his own people were and watched them at their hard labour. He saw an Egyptian beating a Hebrew, one of his own people… (he killed him and had to flee).

וַיְהִי בַּיָּמִים הָהֵם וַיִּגְדַּל מֹשֶׁה וַיֵּצֵא אֶל־אֶחָיו וַיַּרְא בְּסִבְלֹתָם וַיַּרְא אִישׁ מִצְרִי מַכֶּה אִישׁ־עִבְרִי מֵאֶחָיו. (וַיַּךְ אֶת־הַמִּצְרִי וַיִּטְמְנֵהוּ בַּחוֹל... וַיִּבְרַח מֹשֶׁה מִפְּנֵי פַרְעֹה.)

During that long period, the king of Egypt died. The Israelites groaned in their slavery and cried out, and their cry for help because of their slavery went up to God.

וַיְהִי בַיָּמִים הָרַבִּים הָהֵם וַיָּמָת מֶלֶךְ מִצְרַיִם וַיֵּאָנְחוּ בְנֵי־יִשְׂרָאֵל מִן־הָעֲבֹדָה וַיִּזְעָקוּ וַתַּעַל שַׁוְעָתָם אֶל־הָאֱלֹהִים מִן־הָעֲבֹדָה.

Continue on page 13b

Telling the story the rabbinic way – 3

Continued from page 12a

And saw. What did the Eternal One see? God saw that the Israelites had compassion for each other: whoever was the first to complete his quota of bricks would then help the others.

וַיַּרְא.
מָה רָאָה יְיָ? שֶׁהָיוּ מְרַחֲמִים זֶה עַל זֶה. כְּשֶׁהָיָה אֶחָד מֵהֶם מַשְׁלִים סְכוּם הַלְּבֵנִים קֹדֶם חֲבֵרוֹ, הָיָה בָא וּמְסַיֵּעַ לוֹ.

Our plight. *This is the enforced separation of husbands and wives. The Egyptians decreed that the men should sleep in the fields and the women in the cities in order to decrease their offspring. But the Israelite women would warm up food and bring it to their husbands. They would comfort their husbands by saying 'We shall not be enslaved forever; the Holy One will free us.' Then they would come together and have children. Thus our ancestors were redeemed from Egypt due to the merit of the righteous women in that generation.*

אֶת־עָנְיֵנוּ.
זוֹ פְּרִישׁוּת דֶּרֶךְ אֶרֶץ. שֶׁגָּזְרוּ עֲלֵיהֶם הַמִּצְרִים שֶׁיָּלִינוּ הָאֲנָשִׁים בַּשָּׂדֶה וְהַנָּשִׁים בָּעִיר כְּדֵי לְמַעֲטָם בִּפְרִיָּה וּרְבִיָּה. אֶלָּא שֶׁהַנָּשִׁים הָיוּ מְחַמְּמוֹת חַמִּין וּמְבִיאוֹת לְבַעֲלֵיהֶן כָּל־מַאֲכָל וּמִשְׁתֶּה וּמְנַחֲמוֹת אֹתָם וְאוֹמְרוֹת: "לֹא לְעוֹלָם מִשְׁתַּעְבְּדִים בָּנוּ. סוֹף הַקָּדוֹשׁ בָּרוּךְ הוּא גּוֹאֵל אוֹתָנוּ." מִתּוֹךְ כָּךְ בָּאִים עֲלֵיהֶן וּפָרִים וְרָבִים. מִכַּאן שֶׁבִּזְכוּת נָשִׁים צִדְקָנִיּוֹת נִגְאֲלוּ אֲבוֹתֵינוּ מִמִּצְרָיִם.

So the Eternal One brought us out of Egypt with a mighty hand and an outstretched arm, with great terror and with miraculous signs and wonders. Thus taught Rabbi Elimelech of Lizensk: 'At the pronouncement of laws, the Holy Scripture always makes mention of the Exodus from Egypt, and never of the Creation of the world. Why is this? Was not the Creation out of a void a greater miracle than the Exodus? Understand, then, that the Creation, properly speaking, was not a miracle. All nature is in, and subject to, God, and whatever sprang into being at God's behest did so in a natural way. But the Exodus was a wonder, for to deal with the Egyptians according to their merits, it was necessary for the divine aspect of goodness to be suspended in order for evil temporarily to prevail.

וַיּוֹצִאֵנוּ יְהוָה מִמִּצְרַיִם בְּיָד חֲזָקָה וּבִזְרֹעַ נְטוּיָה וּבְמֹרָא גָּדֹל וּבְאֹתוֹת וּבְמֹפְתִים.

Prague, 1526

Continue on page 14a

Telling the story the biblical way – 3

Continued from page 12b

God heard their groaning and remembered the covenant. So God looked on the Israelites and was concerned about them.

וַיִּשְׁמַע אֱלֹהִים אֶת־נַאֲקָתָם וַיִּזְכֹּר אֱלֹהִים אֶת־בְּרִיתוֹ וַיַּרְא אֱלֹהִים אֶת־בְּנֵי יִשְׂרָאֵל וַיֵּדַע אֱלֹהִים.

Now Moses was tending the flock of Jethro his father-in-law, the priest of Midian, and he led the flock to the far side of the desert and came to Horeb, the mountain of God.

וּמֹשֶׁה הָיָה רֹעֶה אֶת־צֹאן יִתְרוֹ חֹתְנוֹ כֹּהֵן מִדְיָן וַיִּנְהַג אֶת־הַצֹּאן אַחַר הַמִּדְבָּר וַיָּבֹא אֶל־הַר הָאֱלֹהִים חֹרֵבָה.

There the angel of the Eternal One appeared to him in flames of fire from within a bush. Moses saw that though the bush was on fire it did not burn up.

וַיֵּרָא מַלְאַךְ יְהוָה אֵלָיו בְּלַבַּת־אֵשׁ מִתּוֹךְ הַסְּנֶה וַיַּרְא וְהִנֵּה הַסְּנֶה בֹּעֵר בָּאֵשׁ וְהַסְּנֶה אֵינֶנּוּ אֻכָּל.

When the Eternal One saw that he had gone over to look, God called to him from within the bush, 'Moses! Moses!' And Moses said, 'Here I am.'

וַיַּרְא יְהוָה כִּי סָר לִרְאוֹת וַיִּקְרָא אֵלָיו אֱלֹהִים מִתּוֹךְ הַסְּנֶה וַיֹּאמֶר מֹשֶׁה, מֹשֶׁה! וַיֹּאמֶר הִנֵּנִי.

Then the Eternal One said, 'I have heard the groaning of the Israelites, whom the Egyptians are enslaving, and I have remembered My covenant.'

וַיֹּאמֶר יְהוָה אֲנִי שָׁמַעְתִּי אֶת־נַאֲקַת בְּנֵי יִשְׂרָאֵל אֲשֶׁר מִצְרַיִם מַעֲבִדִים אֹתָם וָאֶזְכֹּר אֶת־בְּרִיתִי.

'Therefore, say to the Israelite people: "I am the Eternal One and I will release you from Egyptian oppression and I will deliver you from serving them. I will redeem you with an outstretched arm and with great acts and I will take you to be My people and I will be your God that you might know that I am the Eternal One, your God, who will bring you out from Egyptian oppression."'

לָכֵן אֱמֹר לִבְנֵי־יִשְׂרָאֵל: אֲנִי יְהוָה וְהוֹצֵאתִי אֶתְכֶם מִתַּחַת סִבְלֹת מִצְרַיִם וְהִצַּלְתִּי אֶתְכֶם מֵעֲבֹדָתָם וְגָאַלְתִּי אֶתְכֶם בִּזְרוֹעַ נְטוּיָה וּבִשְׁפָטִים גְּדֹלִים. וְלָקַחְתִּי אֶתְכֶם לִי לְעָם וְהָיִיתִי לָכֶם לֵאלֹהִים וִידַעְתֶּם כִּי אֲנִי יְהוָה אֱלֹהֵיכֶם הַמּוֹצִיא אֶתְכֶם מִתַּחַת סִבְלוֹת מִצְרָיִם.

Continue on page 14a

Exodus: chapter **1:** verse(s) 8-9, 11, 14, 15-17, 22; **2:** 1-2, 3-4, 5-6, 7-8, 10, 11, 23, 24-25; **3:** 1, 2, 4, 6; **6:** 5, 6-7.

The plagues

After recounting the story of the Exodus from Egypt, resume here:

No liberation is easy. As evil takes its toll, so does the fight against it. As tyranny brings death and terror to its victims, so the struggle to overthrow it claims its casualties. In the upheaval, persecuted and persecutor, innocent and guilty, all will suffer. There is no redemption without pain.

Our rejoicing at the liberation of our ancestors from Egyptian bondage should be tempered by the memory, not only of their own suffering, but also of that of their oppressors. As we tell the story of the Ten Plagues, each one of them diminishes our cup of joy.

It is customary, at the mention of each plague, to spill one drop of wine

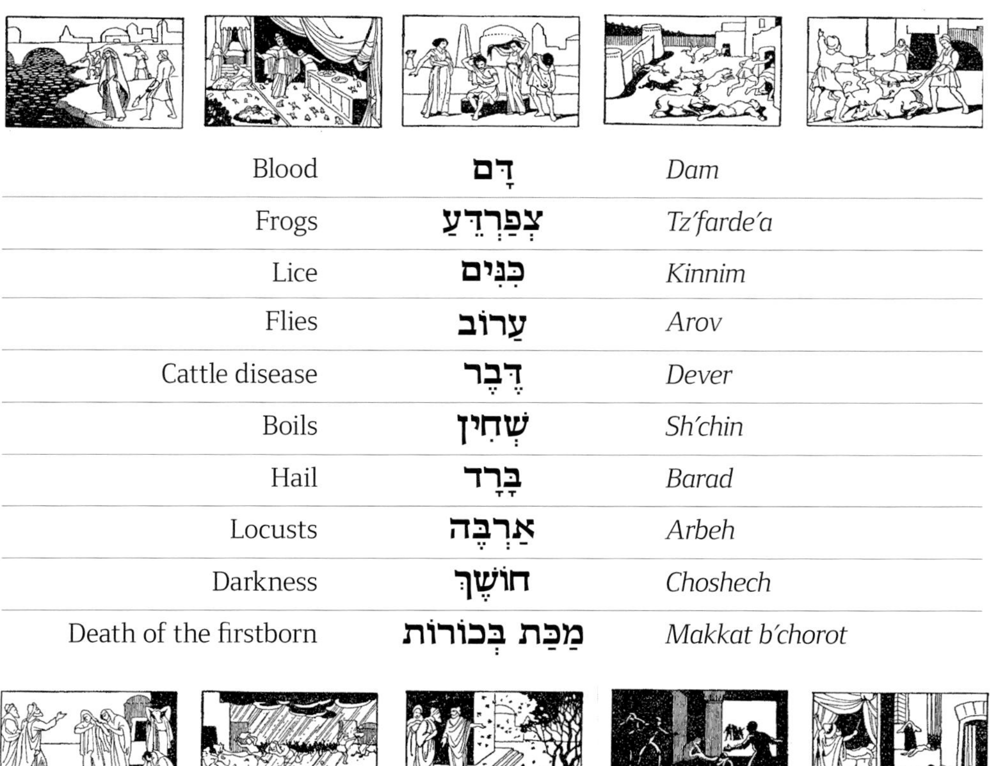

Blood	דָּם	*Dam*
Frogs	צְפַרְדֵּעַ	*Tz'farde'a*
Lice	כִּנִּים	*Kinnim*
Flies	עָרוֹב	*Arov*
Cattle disease	דֶּבֶר	*Dever*
Boils	שְׁחִין	*Sh'chin*
Hail	בָּרָד	*Barad*
Locusts	אַרְבֶּה	*Arbeh*
Darkness	חוֹשֶׁךְ	*Choshech*
Death of the firstborn	מַכַּת בְּכוֹרוֹת	*Makkat b'chorot*

Haggdah l'leyl shimmurim, Frankfurt am Main 1926

Sadly we recall that, as we celebrate our freedom, we do so in a world that is still blighted by many modern plagues. Today we give different names to the plagues that destroy our environment, our quality of life, our dignity, our very lives. Some are new plagues; others have been with us since the beginning of time. Some are external – AIDS and other diseases, tribal hatreds that have escalated into mass killings; acts of terrorism; floods and earthquakes, drought and famine. Others are inside us – plagues of thought and action that we can seek to control or correct.

These are some of the imperfections that trouble our world:

Ignorance that deceives us into hating what we do not understand.

Cynicism that impels us to mock and debase what others hold dear.

Indifference that leads us to neglect and abuse the environment.

Arrogance that inures us to the needs of others.

Insecurity that makes us cowards in the face of criticism.

Envy that narrows our horizons and poisons our relationships with others.

Deceit that causes us to disappoint those who trust us most.

Dogmatism that blinds us to the reality of alternative and sincerely held points of view.

Bigotry that drives us to define people by what they are rather than who they are, leading us to deny equality, respect and opportunity on the basis of superficial differences.

Hardness of heart that condemns us to ignore the feelings and needs of those closest to us.

May we have the strength of mind and body to put an end to the plagues that threaten our lives and endanger our souls.

Our story continues…

When the cup of suffering had run over, Egypt's grip was loosened. On that day, Israel went forth to freedom. They made their way to the Sea of Reeds. Cloud by day, fire by night; God's Presence went before them. But Pharaoh's heart changed yet again – for the oppressors' fury grows as their grip begins to weaken, and in their rage they pursue their victims even to their own destruction. In swift pursuit Pharaoh's troops caught up with the fleeing slaves. Israel stood uncertain: before them the Sea, behind them Egypt's host.

When Israel stood at the edge of the sea, each one said: 'I will not be the first to enter…' While they stood there deliberating, Nachshon ben Amminadav leapt first into the Sea and plunged into its waves. (*Mechilta* to Exodus 14:22)

The Sea did not part for them until they had waded into it up to their noses; only then did it become dry land. (Exodus *Rabbah* 21:10)

The people overcame their fear, as all must in every generation who would be free, trusting in the power of right to conquer might, as it is said:

'Have no fear, for I shall redeem you. I have called you by name, you are Mine. When you pass through the waters I will be with you; and through the rivers, they shall not overwhelm you.' (Isaiah 13:1)

At that time the ministering angels wanted to sing a song of praise to the Holy One, ever to be blessed: but God restrained them, saying 'My creatures are drowning in the sea, and you would sing before Me!' (*Sanhedrin* 39b)

O God, teach us to rejoice in freedom, but not in its cost for us and our enemies. Let there come a day when violence is no more, and we shall be free to rejoice without sadness, to sing without tears.

That day is not yet. Since the Exodus we have known many oppressions and many deliverances. Often we have suffered, often triumphed – and always, as a people, survived. For God, who redeemed Jacob from the hand of one stronger than himself, has been our never-failing strength: as it is said:

'Have no fear, for I am with you; do not despair, for I am your God. I will strengthen you, and help you; I will uphold you with My victorious right hand.' (Isaiah 41:10)

Miriam's song at the Sea of Reeds

And Miriam the prophet, the sister of Aaron, took her timbrel in her hand and she went out. The women followed after her with cymbals and they danced. And Miriam said to them: 'Sing to the Eternal One who has triumphed greatly – horse and rider have been hurled into the sea.' (Exodus 15:19-21)

וַתִּקַּח מִרְיָם הַנְּבִיאָה אֲחוֹת אַהֲרֹן אֶת־הַתֹּף בְּיָדָהּ וַתֵּצֶאןָ כָל־הַנָּשִׁים אַחֲרֶיהָ בְּתֻפִּים וּבִמְחֹלֹת. וַתַּעַן לָהֶם מִרְיָם שִׁירוּ לַיהוָה כִּי־גָאֹה גָּאָה סוּס וְרֹכְבוֹ רָמָה בַיָּם.

♪ Miriam's Song

Miriam was a weaver of unique variety,
The tapestry she wove was one which sang our history.
With every strand and every thread
she crafted her delight,
A woman touched with spirit,
she danced towards the light.

Chorus And the women dancing with their timbrels,
Followed Miriam as she sang her song:
'Sing a song to the One whom we've exalted!'
Miriam and the women danced, they danced the whole night long.

When Miriam stood upon the shores
and gazed across the sea,
The wonder of this miracle
she soon came to believe.
'Whoever thought the sea would part
with an outstretched hand
And we would pass to freedom
and march to the promised land?' *(Chorus)*

And Miriam the prophet
took her timbrel in her hand,
And all the women followed her,
just as she had planned.
Miriam raised her voice in song,
she sang with praise and might,
'We've just lived through a miracle,
we're going to dance all night!' *(Chorus)*

Debbie Friedman

Miriam The Prophet at the Red Sea, Marc Chagall

It would have been enough

How many benefits the Eternal One has granted us!	כַּמָּה מַעֲלוֹת טוֹבוֹת לַמָּקוֹם עָלֵינוּ!
Had God brought us out of Egypt and not supported us in the wilderness – *It would have been enough –**Dayyeinu!***	אִלּוּ הוֹצִיאָנוּ מִמִּצְרַיִם וְלֹא סִפֵּק צָרְכֵּנוּ בַּמִּדְבָּר – **דַּיֵּנוּ!**
Had God supported us in the wilderness and not given us Shabbat –***Dayyeinu!***	אִלּוּ סִפֵּק צָרְכֵּנוּ בַּמִּדְבָּר וְלֹא נָתַן לָנוּ אֶת־הַשַּׁבָּת – **דַּיֵּנוּ!**
Had God given us Shabbat and not given us the Torah – ***Dayyeinu!***	אִלּוּ נָתַן לָנוּ אֶת־הַשַּׁבָּת וְלֹא נָתַן לָנוּ אֶת־הַתּוֹרָה – **דַּיֵּנוּ!**
Had God given us the Torah and not brought us to the land of Israel – ***Dayyeinu!***	אִלּוּ נָתַן לָנוּ אֶת־הַתּוֹרָה וְלֹא הִכְנִיסָנוּ לְאֶרֶץ־יִשְׂרָאֵל – **דַּיֵּנוּ!**
Had God brought us to the land of Israel and not sent us the prophets – ***Dayyeinu!***	אִלּוּ הִכְנִיסָנוּ לְאֶרֶץ־יִשְׂרָאֵל וְלֹא שָׁלַח לָנוּ אֶת־הַנְּבִיאִים – **דַּיֵּנוּ!**
Had God sent us the prophets and not called us to be a light to nations – ***Dayyeinu!***	אִלּוּ שָׁלַח לָנוּ אֶת־הַנְּבִיאִים וְלֹא נְתָנָנוּ לְאוֹר גּוֹיִם – **דַּיֵּנוּ!**
Had God called us to be a light to nations and not sustained us in all the lands of our dispersion – ***Dayyeinu!***	אִלּוּ נְתָנָנוּ לְאוֹר גּוֹיִם וְלֹא הֶחֱיָנוּ בִּתְפוּצוֹתֵינוּ – **דַּיֵּנוּ!**
Had God sustained us in all the lands of our dispersion and not enabled us to return to the land of our ancestors – ***Dayyeinu!***	אִלּוּ הֶחֱיָנוּ בִּתְפוּצוֹתֵינוּ וְלֹא הֱשִׁיבָנוּ לְאֶרֶץ אֲבוֹתֵינוּ – **דַּיֵּנוּ!**
Had God enabled us to return to the land of our ancestors and not enjoined us to perfect the world – ***Dayyeinu!***	אִלּוּ הֱשִׁיבָנוּ לְאֶרֶץ אֲבוֹתֵינוּ וְלֹא צִוָּנוּ לְתַקֵּן עוֹלָמוֹ – **דַּיֵּנוּ!**

♪ *Kammah ma'alot tovot la-makom aleinu!*

Illu hotzi'anu mi-mitzrayim, v'lo sippeik tzorkeinu ba-midbar –	***Dayyeinu!***
Illu sippeik tzorkeinu ba-midbar, v'lo natan lanu et ha-Shabbat –	***Dayyeinu!***
Illu natan lanu et ha-Shabbat, v'lo natan lanu et ha-Torah –	***Dayyeinu!***
Illu natan lanu et ha-Torah, v'lo hichnisanu l'eretz yisra'el –	***Dayyeinu!***
Illu hichnisanu l'eretz yisra'el, v'lo shalach lanu et ha-n'vi'im –	***Dayyeinu!***
Illu shalach lanu et ha-n'vi'im, v'lo n'tananu l'or goyim –	***Dayyeinu!***
Illu n'tananu l'or goyim, v'lo hecheyanu bit'futzateinu –	***Dayyeinu!***
Illu hecheyanu bit'futzateinu, v'lo heshivanu l'eretz avoteinu –	***Dayyeinu!***
Illu heshivanu l'eretz avoteinu, v'lo tzivvanu l'takkein olamo –	***Dayyeinu!***

♪ This folk song, based on a Yiddish original, reminds us we must be active in seeking freedom. The Hebrew for freedom is *d'ror,* which also means 'a swallow'

Donna, Donna

On a wagon, bound for market,
There's a calf with a mournful eye.
High above him flies a swallow,
♪ Winging freely through the sky.

Chorus
How the winds are laughing,
They laugh with all their might;
Laugh and laugh the whole day through,
And half the summer's night.
Donna donna donna donna,
Donna donna donna don.

'Stop complaining,' said the farmer,
'Who told you a calf to be?
'Why don't you have wings to fly with,
'Like the swallow so proud and free?'

Calves are easily bound and slaughtered,
Never knowing the reason why.
But whoever treasures freedom,
Like the swallow must learn to fly.

Trieste, 1864

How much more should we be thankful for the countless benefits God has give us! For God brought us out of Egypt, supported us in the wilderness, gave us the Sabbath, gave us the Torah, brought us to the land of Israel, sent us the prophets, called us to be a light to nations, sustained us in all the lands of our dispersion, enabled us to return to the land of our ancestors and enjoined us to perfect the world.

עַל אַחַת כַּמָּה וְכַמָּה טוֹבָה כְּפוּלָה וּמְכֻפֶּלֶת לַמָּקוֹם עָלֵינוּ! שֶׁהוֹצִיאָנוּ מִמִּצְרָיִם, וְסִפֵּק צָרְכֵּנוּ בַּמִּדְבָּר וְנָתַן לָנוּ אֶת־הַשַּׁבָּת, וְנָתַן לָנוּ אֶת־הַתּוֹרָה, וְהִכְנִיסָנוּ לְאֶרֶץ־יִשְׂרָאֵל, וְשָׁלַח לָנוּ אֶת־הַנְּבִיאִים, וּנְתָנָנוּ לְאוֹר גּוֹיִם, וְהֶחֱיָנוּ בְּכָל־תְּפוּצָתֵנוּ, וְהֱשִׁיבָנוּ לְאֶרֶץ אֲבוֹתֵינוּ, וְצִוָּנוּ לְתַקֵּן עוֹלָמוֹ.

The glasses are raised

Therefore we should thank, bless and praise beyond measure the One who performed all these wonders for our ancestors and for us; who led us from oppression to freedom, from sadness to joy, from grieving to celebration, from darkness to light, from slavery to redemption. Let us therefore sing a new song to God: *Halleluyah*!

לְפִיכָךְ אֲנַחְנוּ חַיָּבִין לְהוֹדוֹת, לְהַלֵּל, לְשַׁבֵּחַ, לְפָאֵר, לְרוֹמֵם, לְהַדֵּר, לְבָרֵךְ, לְעַלֵּה וּלְקַלֵּס, לְמִי שֶׁעָשָׂה לַאֲבוֹתֵינוּ וְלָנוּ אֶת כָּל הַנִּסִּים הָאֵלּוּ, הוֹצִיאָנוּ מֵעַבְדוּת לְחֵרוּת, מִיָּגוֹן לְשִׂמְחָה, מֵאֵבֶל לְיוֹם טוֹב, מֵאֲפֵלָה לְאוֹר גָּדוֹל, וּמִשִּׁעְבּוּד לִגְאֻלָּה. וְנֹאמַר לְפָנָיו שִׁירָה חֲדָשָׁה: הַלְלוּיָהּ!

The glasses are lowered

Siegmund Forst, New York, 1959

The Hebrew word for Egypt, *mitzrayim,* means a tight spot or a narrow strait where we feel 'boxed in'.

'One day, a few days after the liberation, I walked through the country past flowering meadows, for miles and miles, toward the market town near the camp. Larks rose to the sky and I could hear their joyous song. There was no one to be seen for miles around, there was nothing but the wide earth and sky and the larks' jubilation and the freedom of space. I stopped, looked around, and up to the sky – and then I went down on my knees. At that moment there was very little I knew of myself or the world – I had but one sentence in mind – always the same: 'I called to the Eternal One from my prison and God answered me in the freedom of space.' (Psalm 118:5)

How long I knelt there and repeated this sentence, memory can no longer recall. But I know that on that day, in that hour, my new life started. Step for step I progressed, until I again became a human being.'

Viktor Frankl, *Man's Search for Meaning, Lessons from a Concentration Camp.*

Venice, 1601

We were strangers in Egypt and Kiev, we were foreigners in Babylon and Berlin.
We were outsiders and wanderers in Spain and Poland and France.
We looked at the citizens of those lands with the dark, pleading eyes of the alien,
Our hearts beat the hesitant beat of those without rights, fearful and uncertain.
And so we pray, help us to remember the heart of the stranger when we walk in freedom.
Help us to be fair and upright in all our dealings with all people.
Oh burn and brand the lesson of all the years and all the lands in our hearts.
Eternal One, make us forever strangers to discrimination and injustice.

Anon.

Hallel הַלֵּל

From Psalm 113

Halleluyah! Give praise, O servants of the Eternal One;
praise the name of the Eternal One.
Let God's name be praised, both now and for ever.
From the rising of the sun to its setting
let God be praised.
Exalted above the nations is Israel's God
whose glory is above the heavens.
Who can be compared to our God, who is enthroned on high,
And yet looks down on heaven and the earth?
Who raises the poor from the dust
and lifts the needy from the mire,
To give them a place among the great,
Among the leaders of the people.
Halleluyah!

הַלְלוּיָהּ! הַלְלוּ עַבְדֵי יְהֹוָה
הַלְלוּ אֶת־שֵׁם יְהֹוָה.
יְהִי שֵׁם יְהֹוָה מְבֹרָךְ
מֵעַתָּה וְעַד־עוֹלָם.
מִמִּזְרַח־שֶׁמֶשׁ עַד־מְבוֹאוֹ
מְהֻלָּל שֵׁם יְהֹוָה.
רָם עַל־כָּל־גּוֹיִם יְהֹוָה
עַל הַשָּׁמַיִם כְּבוֹדוֹ.
מִי כַּיהֹוָה אֱלֹהֵינוּ
הַמַּגְבִּיהִי לָשָׁבֶת.
הַמַּשְׁפִּילִי לִרְאוֹת
בַּשָּׁמַיִם וּבָאָרֶץ.
מְקִימִי מֵעָפָר דָּל
מֵאַשְׁפֹּת יָרִים אֶבְיוֹן.
לְהוֹשִׁיבִי עִם־נְדִיבִים
עִם נְדִיבֵי עַמּוֹ. **הַלְלוּיָהּ!**

Halleluyah!
Hallelu avdei Adonai, hallelu et sheim Adonai.
Y'hi sheim Adonai m'vorach mei'atah v'ad olam.
Mi-mizrach shemesh ad m'vo'o m'hullal sheim Adonai.
Ram al kol goyim Adonai al ha-shamayim k'vodo.
Mi k'Adonai eloheinu ha-magbihi la'shavet.
Ha-mashpili lir'ot ba-shamayim u-va-aretz.
M'kimi mei'afar dal mei-ashpot yarim evyon.
L'hoshivi im n'divim im n'divei ammo.
Halleluyah!

Why do we recite Hallel in two parts – the first part (Psalm 113 and 114) before the meal and the second (Psalm 117 and 118) after it? The first half is about the Exodus from Egypt and the past. The second is about the future of the Jewish people and the world. (The pity is that many Jews end their *Seder* with the meal, happily celebrating our past, but with no time to express hope for our future.)

Michel Kichka, King David and the Levite Band

Michel Kichka ©

Hallelu hallelu hallelu,
Kol ha-n'shamah t'hallel yah -
Hallelu Halleluyah!

הַלְלוּ הַלְלוּ הַלְלוּ
כֹּל הַנְּשָׁמָה תְּהַלֵּל יָהּ
הַלְלוּ הַלְלוּיָהּ.

Let us give praise – let every soul praise the Eternal One – *Halleluyah!*
(From Psalm 150)

Psalm 114

When Israel went forth from Egypt
The house of Jacob from an alien people,
Judah became God's sanctuary
Israel accepted God's rule.
The sea looked and fled
The Jordan turned back on its course.
The mountains skipped like rams
The hills like young lambs.
What makes you flee, O sea?
Why do you turn back, O Jordan?
O mountains, why do you skip like rams
You hills, like young lambs?
Tremble, O earth, before the Eternal One,
Before the God of Jacob,
Who turns the rock into a pool of water
The flinty rock into a fountain.

בְּצֵאת יִשְׂרָאֵל מִמִּצְרָיִם
בֵּית יַעֲקֹב מֵעַם לֹעֵז.
הָיְתָה יְהוּדָה לְקָדְשׁוֹ
יִשְׂרָאֵל מַמְשְׁלוֹתָיו.
הַיָּם רָאָה וַיָּנֹס
הַיַּרְדֵּן יִסֹּב לְאָחוֹר.
הֶהָרִים רָקְדוּ כְאֵילִים
גְּבָעוֹת כִּבְנֵי־צֹאן.
מַה־לְּךָ הַיָּם כִּי תָנוּס
הַיַּרְדֵּן תִּסֹּב לְאָחוֹר?
הֶהָרִים תִּרְקְדוּ כְאֵילִים
גְּבָעוֹת כִּבְנֵי־צֹאן?
מִלִּפְנֵי אָדוֹן חוּלִי אָרֶץ
מִלִּפְנֵי אֱלוֹהַּ יַעֲקֹב.
הַהֹפְכִי הַצּוּר אֲגַם־מָיִם
חַלָּמִישׁ לְמַעְיְנוֹ־מָיִם.

B'tzeit yisra'el mi-mitzrayim beit ya'akov mei'am lo'eiz
hay'tah y'hudah l'kodsho yisra'el mamsh'lotav
ha-yam ra'ah vayanos ha-yardein yissov l'achor
he-harim rakdu ch'eilim g'va'ot kiv'nei tzon.

Mah l'cha ha-yam ki tanus ha-yardein tissov l'achor?
he-harim tirk'du ch'eilim g'va'ot kiv'nei tzon?
mi-lifnei adon chuli aretz, mi-lifnei elo'ah ya'akov
ha-hofchi ha-tzur agam mayim challamish l'may'no mayim.

♪ God of might
(To the tune of *Addir Hu*)

God of might, God of right
Rock of our salvation
Unto You still we do
Offer adoration.
Since Your hand from
Egypt's land
Led Your chosen nation.

God of all, when we call,
On Your love unending
Save and hear, O be near,
Unto us extending
Power benign, grace divine
In our hearts descending.

Mighty God, by Your word
Freedom first was given.
Now as then, let again
Bonds and chains be riven.
You we trust, wise and just,
God of earth and heaven.
Gustav Gottheil

Dieses Lied wird am andern Osterabend / anstat dessen/welches/also(Dann dir geziembts) anfängt/gesungen.

Cantio hæc ſecundis ferys Paſchalibus, loco ejus; quæ à capite, Ky lo Nach, Ky lo Jach, incipit, canitur,

MAgnificus (qui eſt) ille ædificabit domum ſuam brevi, cito in diebus noſtris ocyus; (Ah) ædifica, ædifica, ædifica, ædifica domum tuam brevi:

Electus(qui eſt)ille ædificabit domum ſuam brevi, cito in diebus noſtris ocyus; (Ah) ædifica, ædifica, ædifica, ædifica domnm tuam brevi:

אדיר הוא יבנה ב
ביתו בקרוב במהרה בימינו
בקרוב אל בנה בנה בנה
בנה ביתך בקרוב:
בחור הוא יבנה ביתו
בקרוב במהרה בימינו בק
בקרוב אל בנה בנה בנה
בנה ביתך בקרוב:

R 3 Magnus

Addir Hu, Königsberg, 1644

B'chol dor va-dor בְּכָל דּוֹר וָדוֹר

In every generation… Here is the essential purpose of this night: to experience the *Seder* as though it were happening to us and to tell it to the next generation:

בְּכָל דּוֹר וָדוֹר חַיָּב אָדָם לִרְאוֹת אֶת עַצְמוֹ כְּאִלּוּ הוּא יָצָא מִמִּצְרַיִם, שֶׁנֶּאֱמַר: "וְהִגַּדְתָּ לְבִנְךָ בַּיּוֹם הַהוּא לֵאמֹר: בַּעֲבוּר זֶה עָשָׂה יְיָ לִי בְּצֵאתִי מִמִּצְרָיִם." לֹא אֶת־אֲבוֹתֵינוּ בִּלְבַד גָּאַל הַקָּדוֹשׁ בָּרוּךְ הוּא, אֶלָּא אַף אוֹתָנוּ גָּאַל עִמָּהֶם.

In each generation we should all imagine that we ourselves came out of Egypt, as we read: 'You shall tell your child on that day: It is in commemoration of what the Eternal One did for me when I came out of Egypt.' For the Holy One, ever to be praised, redeemed not only our ancestors, but us along with them.

The second glass כּוֹס שֵׁנִי

We raise our glasses in remembrance of the second promise of redemption, as it is said:

"וְהִצַּלְתִּי אֶתְכֶם מֵעֲבֹדָתָם."

I will deliver you from serving them.

בָּרוּךְ אַתָּה יְיָ אֱלֹהֵינוּ מֶלֶךְ הָעוֹלָם, אֲשֶׁר גְּאָלָנוּ וְגָאַל אֶת־אֲבוֹתֵינוּ מִמִּצְרָיִם, וְהִגִּיעָנוּ לַלַּיְלָה הַזֶּה, לֶאֱכָל־בּוֹ מַצָּה וּמָרוֹר. כֵּן יְיָ אֱלֹהֵינוּ וֵאלֹהֵי אֲבוֹתֵינוּ, הַגִּיעֵנוּ לְמוֹעֲדִים וְלִרְגָלִים אֲחֵרִים, הַבָּאִים לִקְרָאתֵנוּ לְשָׁלוֹם, שְׂמֵחִים בְּבִנְיַן עִירֶךָ, וְשָׂשִׂים בַּעֲבוֹדָתֶךָ. וְנוֹדֶה לְךָ שִׁיר חָדָשׁ עַל גְּאֻלָּתֵנוּ וְעַל פְּדוּת נַפְשֵׁנוּ. בָּרוּךְ אַתָּה יְיָ גָּאַל יִשְׂרָאֵל.
בָּרוּךְ אַתָּה יְיָ אֱלֹהֵינוּ מֶלֶךְ הָעוֹלָם, בּוֹרֵא פְּרִי הַגָּפֶן.

We praise You, Eternal God, Sovereign of the universe, who have redeemed us and our ancestors from Egypt, and enabled us to reach this night, to celebrate our freedom by eating *Matzah* and *Maror*. Grant, Eternal God and God of our ancestors, that we may reach yet other holy days and festivals, living in peace, building Your City in gladness, and serving You in joy. Then we shall sing to You a new song of praise for our redemption from oppression and for our inner freedom.
We praise You, O God, Redeemer of Israel.
We praise You, Eternal God, Sovereign of the universe, Creator of the fruit of the vine.

Baruch atah Adonai eloheinu melech ha-olam asher g'alanu v'ga'al et avoteinu mi-mitzrayim, v'higgi'anu la-lailah ha-zeh, le'echol bo matzah u-maror. Kein Adonai eloheinu veilohei avoteinu, haggi'einu l'mo'adim v'lirgalim acheirim ha-ba'im likrateinu l'shalom, s'meichim b'vinyan irecha, v'sasim ba-avodatecha. V'nodah l'cha shir chadash al g'ullateinu v'al p'dut nafsheinu. Baruch atah Adonai, ga'al yisra'el.
Baruch atah Adonai eloheinu melech ha-olam borei p'ri ha-gafen.

Lean to the left and drink the second glass of wine

Maggid

The courage to let go of the door, the handle.
The courage to shed the familiar walls whose very
stains and leaks are comfortable as the little moles
of the upper arm; stains that recall a feast,
a child's naughtiness, a loud blistering storm
that slapped the roof hard, pouring through.

The courage to abandon the graves dug into the hill,
the small bones of children and the brittle bones
of the old whose marrow hunger had stolen;
the courage to desert the tree planted and only
begun to bear; the riverside where promises were
shaped; the street where their empty pots were broken.

The courage to leave the place whose language you learned
as early as your own, whose customs however
dangerous or demeaning, bind you like a halter
you have learned to pull inside, to move your load;
the land fertile with the blood spilled on it;
the roads mapped and annotated for survival.

The courage to walk out of the pain that is known
into the pain that cannot be imagined,
mapless, walking into the wilderness, going
barefoot with a canteen into the desert;
stuffed in the stinking hold of a rotting ship
sailing off the map into dragons' mouths.

Cathay, India, Serbia, *goldeneh medina*,
leaving bodies by the way like abandoned treasure.
So they walked out of Egypt. So they bribed their way
out of Russia under loaves of straw; so they steamed
out of the bloody smoking charnelhouse of Europe
on overloaded freighters forbidden all ports –

out of pain into death or freedom or a different
painful dignity, into squalor and politics.
We Jews are all born of wanderers, with shoes
under our pillows and a memory of blood that is ours
raining down. We honor only those Jews who changed
tonight, those who chose the desert over bondage,

who walked into the strange and became strangers
and gave birth to children who could look down
on them standing on their shoulders for having
been slaves. We honor those who let go of everything
but freedom, who ran, who revolted, who fought,
who became other by saving themselves.

Marge Piercy

Pesach פֶּסַח

The Paschal Lamb

The leader holds up the Bone

רַבָּן גַּמְלִיאֵל הָיָה אוֹמֵר, ”כָּל שֶׁלֹּא אָמַר שְׁלֹשָׁה דְּבָרִים אֵלּוּ בַּפֶּסַח, לֹא יָצָא יְדֵי חוֹבָתוֹ, וְאֵלּוּ הֵן, פֶּסַח, מַצָּה, וּמָרוֹר.”

Rabban Gamliel used to say: ‘If, on the Passover, you do not explain these three things, you have not fulfilled your obligation: *Pesach*, *Matzah* and *Maror*.’

פֶּסַח שֶׁהָיוּ אֲבוֹתֵינוּ אוֹכְלִים בִּזְמַן שֶׁבֵּית הַמִּקְדָּשׁ קַיָּם, עַל שׁוּם מָה? עַל שׁוּם שֶׁפָּסַח הַמָּקוֹם עַל בָּתֵּי אֲבוֹתֵינוּ בְּמִצְרַיִם. שֶׁנֶּאֱמַר: ”וַאֲמַרְתֶּם זֶבַח־פֶּסַח הוּא לַיהֹוָה אֲשֶׁר פָּסַח עַל־בָּתֵּי בְנֵי־יִשְׂרָאֵל בְּמִצְרַיִם בְּנָגְפּוֹ אֶת־מִצְרַיִם וְאֶת־בָּתֵּינוּ הִצִּיל.”

Why, in the days when the Temple still stood, did our ancestors eat at this time a ‘Passover’ lamb? Because the Holy One, ever to be blessed, passed over the houses of our ancestors in Egypt, as it is said: ‘It is a Passover offering to God, who passed over the houses of the Israelites in Egypt, striking the Egyptians but sparing our houses.’

Washing the hands רָחְצָה

At this point, prior to eating *Matzah*, it is traditional at some *Sedarim* to bring water for the washing of the hands.

בָּרוּךְ אַתָּה יְיָ אֱלֹהֵינוּ מֶלֶךְ הָעוֹלָם, אֲשֶׁר קִדְּשָׁנוּ בְּמִצְוֹתָיו, וְצִוָּנוּ עַל נְטִילַת יָדָיִם.

We praise you, Eternal God, Sovereign of the Universe: You sanctify us by Your commandments and enjoin us to wash our hands.

Baruch atah Adonai eloheinu melech ha-olam asher kidd'shanu b'mitzvotav v'tzivvanu al n'tilat yadayim.

Our re-telling of the Exodus story has brought us from slavery to freedom, but it has also brought us into the wilderness, a dry and dangerous place with no water.

וַיָּבֹאוּ בְנֵי־יִשְׂרָאֵל כָּל־הָעֵדָה מִדְבַּר־צִן בַּחֹדֶשׁ הָרִאשׁוֹן וַיֵּשֶׁב הָעָם בְּקָדֵשׁ וַתָּמָת שָׁם מִרְיָם וַתִּקָּבֵר שָׁם.

וְלֹא־הָיָה מַיִם לָעֵדָה וַיִּקָּהֲלוּ עַל־מֹשֶׁה וְעַל־אַהֲרֹן.

1. In the first month, the whole congregation of the children of Israel came to the wilderness of Zin. The people dwelt in Kadesh. Miriam died and was buried there.
2. And there was no water for the community and the people gathered against Moses and Aaron. (Numbers 20:1-2)

Jewish tradition combined these two verses to create the story of Miriam's Well. The fact that the Israelites were without water as soon as Miriam died led the sages to conclude that Miriam had been responsible for providing water for them during their journey through the wilderness.

This story teaches that Miriam played a vital role in sustaining our ancestors as they left Egypt and travelled to freedom. Therefore it is appropriate to fill a cup with water and place Miriam's Cup (*cos shel Mir'yam*) alongside that which awaits Elijah.

Matzah מַצָּה

Unleavened Bread

The leader holds up the *Matzah*

Why do we eat this unleavened bread? Because our ancestors did not have time to let their dough ferment before the true Ruler, the Holy One, ever to be blessed, was revealed to them and redeemed them, as it is said: 'They baked the dough they had brought out of Egypt into cakes of unleavened bread, for they were driven out of Egypt so that they could not delay to prepare food for themselves.'

מַצָּה זוֹ שֶׁאָנוּ אוֹכְלִים, עַל שׁוּם מָה? עַל שׁוּם שֶׁלֹּא הִסְפִּיק בְּצֵקָם שֶׁל אֲבוֹתֵינוּ לְהַחֲמִיץ עַד שֶׁנִּגְלָה עֲלֵיהֶם מֶלֶךְ מַלְכֵי הַמְּלָכִים הַקָּדוֹשׁ בָּרוּךְ הוּא וּגְאָלָם. שֶׁנֶּאֱמַר: "וַיֹּאפוּ אֶת־הַבָּצֵק אֲשֶׁר הוֹצִיאוּ מִמִּצְרַיִם עֻגֹת מַצּוֹת כִּי לֹא חָמֵץ כִּי־גֹרְשׁוּ מִמִּצְרַיִם וְלֹא יָכְלוּ לְהִתְמַהְמֵהַּ וְגַם־צֵדָה לֹא־עָשׂוּ לָהֶם."

We praise You, Eternal God, Sovereign of the universe: You cause the earth to bring forth bread.

בָּרוּךְ אַתָּה יְיָ אֱלֹהֵינוּ מֶלֶךְ הָעוֹלָם, הַמּוֹצִיא לֶחֶם מִן הָאָרֶץ.

Baruch atah Adonai eloheinu melech ha-olam ha-motzi lechem min ha-aretz.

We praise You, Eternal God, Sovereign of the universe: You sanctify us by Your commandments and enjoin us to eat unleavened bread.

בָּרוּךְ אַתָּה יְיָ אֱלֹהֵינוּ מֶלֶךְ הָעוֹלָם, אֲשֶׁר קִדְּשָׁנוּ בְּמִצְוֹתָיו, וְצִוָּנוּ עַל אֲכִילַת מַצָּה.

Baruch atah Adonai eloheinu melech ha-olam asher kidd'shanu b'mitzvotav v'tzivvanu al achilat matzah.

All take a piece of *Matzah* and, leaning to the left, eat it

Passover Night 1942

not a crumb of leavened
or unleavened bread
and no manna fell

no water sprang out
of the bunker's wall
the last potato was gone

we sat and munched
chunks of potato peel
more bitter than herbs
we didn't dare to sing
and open the door
for Elijah

we huddled and prayed
while pillars of cloud
massed over our heads
and pillars of fire
loomed like blazing traps

Yala Korwin

Miklos Adler, A Survivors *Haggadah,* 2000

Pesach 1944

The Jewish inmates of the concentration camp at Bergen-Belsen did not have *Matzah* for the observance of Passover in 1944. Although pious Jews in the camp had decided to fast on the festival, the rabbis who were among them decreed that the eating of leaven would be permissible, provided the following prayer be recited before meals:

'Our Father in heaven, behold it is evident and known to Thee that it is our desire to do Thy will and to celebrate the festival of Passover by eating *Matzah* and by observing the prohibition of *Chameitz*. But our heart is pained that the enslavement prevents us and we are in danger of our lives. Behold we are prepared and ready to fulfil Thy commandment 'And ye shall live by them, and not die by them…' Therefore our prayer to Thee is that Thou mayest keep us alive and preserve us and redeem us speedily so that we may observe Thy statutes and do Thy will and serve Thee with a perfect heart. Amen.'

Maror מָרוֹר

Bitter Herbs

The leader holds up the *Maror*

Why do we eat these bitter herbs? Because the Egyptians embittered the life of our ancestors in Egypt, as it is said: 'They made their life bitter through hard labour with clay and bricks, and all kinds of work in the fields; for they were ruthless in the slave-labour they imposed on them.'

מָרוֹר זֶה שֶׁאָנוּ אוֹכְלִים עַל שׁוּם מָה? עַל שׁוּם שֶׁמֵּרְרוּ הַמִּצְרִים אֶת חַיֵּי אֲבוֹתֵינוּ בְּמִצְרָיִם. שֶׁנֶּאֱמַר: "וַיְמָרְרוּ אֶת־חַיֵּיהֶם בַּעֲבֹדָה קָשָׁה בְּחֹמֶר וּבִלְבֵנִים וּבְכָל־עֲבֹדָה בַּשָּׂדֶה אֵת כָּל־עֲבֹדָתָם אֲשֶׁר־עָבְדוּ בָהֶם בְּפָרֶךְ."

We praise You, Eternal God, Sovereign of the universe: You sanctify us by Your commandments and enjoin us to eat bitter herbs.

בָּרוּךְ אַתָּה יְיָ אֱלֹהֵינוּ מֶלֶךְ הָעוֹלָם, אֲשֶׁר קִדְּשָׁנוּ בְּמִצְוֹתָיו, וְצִוָּנוּ עַל אֲכִילַת מָרוֹר.

Baruch atah Adonai eloheinu melech ha-olam asher kidd'shanu b'mitzvotav v'tzivvanu al achilat maror.

All take a piece of *Maror*, dip it in *Charoset*, and eat it

The Hillel sandwich

This is what Hillel used to do when the Temple still stood: he would combine the paschal lamb with unleavened bread and bitter herbs and eat them together to fulfil the verse: 'with unleavened bread and bitter herbs shall they eat it.'

כֵּן עָשָׂה הִלֵּל בִּזְמַן שֶׁבֵּית הַמִּקְדָּשׁ הָיָה קַיָּם: הָיָה כּוֹרֵךְ מַצָּה וּמָרוֹר וְאוֹכֵל בְּיַחַד לְקַיֵּם מַה שֶּׁנֶּאֱמַר "עַל מַצּוֹת וּמְרֹרִים יֹאכְלֻהוּ."

The Hillel sandwich – *Maror* and *Charoset* between two pieces of *Matzah* – is eaten

Shulchan Oreich

The Meal

Questions & answers

Why are the following part of our *Seder*?

THE BONE: 'When the Temple still stood…' Almost two thousand years have passed since sacrifices were offered in Jerusalem. The bone on the *Seder* plate recalls this ancient form of worship, reminding us of our connection with our biblical ancestors and our recognition that, although the outward form of our worship may have changed, the values which underpin our religious heritage remain the same, then as now: the quest for freedom and justice.

THE EGG: *Pesach* is a springtime festival and the egg is a symbol of this time of year. Traditionally, the egg represents the priests' festival offering, but it is also a sign of rebirth. The *Karpas* brought to mind the manifestations of spring around us; let the new life represented by the egg awaken within us new strength, new hope, new joy.

SALT WATER: The salt water, in which the parsley has already been dipped, symbolises the sweat and tears of the Israelites as they suffered under Egyptian bondage. At many *Sedarim*, the custom is to begin the meal with egg in salt water. This is most likely to have originated in our ancestors' wish not to waste food, so having served their symbolic purpose, these items would be eaten!

CHAROSET: This sweet paste reminds us by its appearance of the clay and straw with which our ancestors were forced to make bricks for Pharaoh's building projects in Egypt. By its sweet taste, it softens, but does not remove, the bitter memory of their slavery.

LEANING: With the custom of leaning at the *Seder,* we are emulating the Romans, who ruled Judea at the time the idea of the *Seder* was being developed. At their banquets, they would recline on couches, leaning on their left arms to keep their right hands free for food. So our leaning is a way of celebrating our freedom.

Afikoman

The *Afikoman* is best known as the piece of *Matzah* that is hidden *(tzafun)* and searched for by the children. Perhaps this is another device to sustain the children's interest, for the finder is usually awarded a prize.

Tha *Afikoman* is a source of speculation. The answer to the wise child was that 'one does not conclude the meal with the *Afikoman*.' But what exactly did that law forbid? Was it to move on from one *Seder* to another, or to some kind of after-dinner entertainment? Was it to end the *Seder* meal with a dessert or savoury which would take away the lingering flavour of the symbolic dishes, especially the *Matzah*?

Whatever may be the true origin of the word, it came to be applied to a piece of *Matzah* that is eaten – as a substitute for the forbidden food or action. It is eaten at the very end of the meal, so that the flavour, like our yearning for freedom, may linger in our mouths when the *Seder* is over.

Now the *Seder* moves from telling the story of liberation from Egypt towards our hope and search for redemption in the future. But first we must give thanks for the meal we have just eaten.

Bareich בָּרֵךְ

Thanksgiving for the Meal

From this point onwards, the pages of the *Haggadah* run in consecutive numerical sequence

The glasses are refilled

The Thanksgiving for the Meal can take a number of forms. Following the version offered on this page, continue on page 30. Alternatively, the complete Thanksgiving for the Meal begins on page 25 and also ends on page 30.

Shorter version:

We praise You, Eternal One, our God, Sovereign of the universe, whose goodness sustains the whole world. With grace, love and compassion You provide food for all Your creatures, for Your love is everlasting. Through Your great goodness we have never lacked our daily bread; may we always have sufficient, for Your great name's sake. Your goodness is the source of sustenance for all who live. We praise You, O God, Provider of food for all.

בָּרוּךְ אַתָּה יְיָ, אֱלֹהֵינוּ מֶלֶךְ הָעוֹלָם,
הַזָּן אֶת הָעוֹלָם כֻּלּוֹ בְּטוּבוֹ בְּחֵן
בְּחֶסֶד וּבְרַחֲמִים, הוּא נוֹתֵן לֶחֶם לְכָל
בָּשָׂר כִּי לְעוֹלָם חַסְדּוֹ. וּבְטוּבוֹ הַגָּדוֹל
תָּמִיד לֹא חָסַר לָנוּ, וְאַל יֶחְסַר לָנוּ
מָזוֹן לְעוֹלָם וָעֶד. בַּעֲבוּר שְׁמוֹ הַגָּדוֹל,
כִּי הוּא זָן וּמְפַרְנֵס לַכֹּל וּמֵטִיב לַכֹּל,
וּמֵכִין מָזוֹן לְכָל בְּרִיּוֹתָיו אֲשֶׁר בָּרָא.
בָּרוּךְ אַתָּה יְיָ, הַזָּן אֶת הַכֹּל.

Baruch atah Adonai eloheinu melech ha-olam ha-zan et ha-olam kullo b'tuvo b'chein b'chesed u-v'rachamim hu notein lechem l'chol basar ki l'olam chasdo u-v'tuvo ha-gadol tamid lo chasar lanu v'al yechsar lanu mazon l'olam va-ed ba'avur sh'mo ha-gadol ki hu zan u-m'farneis la-kol u-meitiv la-kol u-meichin mazon l'chol b'riyyotav asher bara. Baruch atah Adonai ha-zan et ha-kol.

Or this *Ladino* version:

We have eaten and drunk; let us thank the holy God, ever to be praised, who gives us bread to eat, and clothes to wear, and years to live. May things always get better, never worse, and may the Creator's goodness towards us never cease.

Ya comimos y bevimos, y al Dio santo Barukh Hu u-Barukh Shemo bendishimos; que mos diõ y mos dara pan para comer y panyos para vestir, y anyos para bivir. Siempre mejor, nunca peor, nunca mos manke la meza del Criador.

Continue on page 30

Full Thanksgiving for the Meal

The complete version of the Thanksgiving for the Meal begins here

A Song of Degrees.
When God restored the exiles to Zion, it was like a dream. Then our mouths were filled with laughter, our tongues with joyful song. Then they said among the nations: 'God has done great things for them.' God has done great things for us, and we rejoice. Restore our fortune, O God, as streams revive the desert. Then those who have sown in tears shall reap in joy. Those who go forth weeping, carrying bags of seeds, shall come home with shouts, laden with sheaves. (Psalm 126)

שִׁיר הַמַּעֲלוֹת
בְּשׁוּב יְהוָה אֶת־שִׁיבַת צִיּוֹן הָיִינוּ כְּחֹלְמִים.
אָז יִמָּלֵא שְׂחוֹק פִּינוּ וּלְשׁוֹנֵנוּ רִנָּה אָז יֹאמְרוּ בַגּוֹיִם הִגְדִּיל יְהוָה לַעֲשׂוֹת עִם־אֵלֶּה.
הִגְדִּיל יְהוָה לַעֲשׂוֹת עִמָּנוּ הָיִינוּ שְׂמֵחִים.
שׁוּבָה יְהוָה אֶת־שְׁבִיתֵנוּ כַּאֲפִיקִים בַּנֶּגֶב.
הַזֹּרְעִים בְּדִמְעָה בְּרִנָּה יִקְצֹרוּ.
הָלוֹךְ יֵלֵךְ וּבָכֹה נֹשֵׂא מֶשֶׁךְ־הַזָּרַע
בֹּא־יָבוֹא בְרִנָּה נֹשֵׂא אֲלֻמֹּתָיו.

Shir ha-ma'alot b'shuv Adonai et shivat tziyyon hayinu k'cholmim. Az yimmalei s'chok pinu u-l'shoneinu rinnah. Az yomru va-goyim higdil Adonai la'asot im eileh. Higdil Adonai la'asot immanu hayinu s'meichim. Shuvah Adonai et sh'viteinu ka'afikim ba-negev. Ha-zor'im b'dim'ah b'rinnah yiktzoru. Haloch yeilech u-vachoh nosei meshech ha-zara bo yavo v'rinnah nosei alumotav.

Friends, let us praise God.
Praised be God's name, now and for ever.
Let us praise our God of whose abundance we have eaten.
We praise our God of whose abundance we have eaten, and by whose goodness we live.
Blessed be God and God's name.

חֲבֵרִים וַחֲבֵרוֹת נְבָרֵךְ.
יְהִי שֵׁם יְיָ מְבֹרָךְ מֵעַתָּה וְעַד עוֹלָם.
נְבָרֵךְ אֱלֹהֵינוּ שֶׁאָכַלְנוּ מִשֶּׁלּוֹ.
בָּרוּךְ אֱלֹהֵינוּ שֶׁאָכַלְנוּ מִשֶּׁלּוֹ וּבְטוּבוֹ חָיִינוּ.
בָּרוּךְ הוּא וּבָרוּךְ שְׁמוֹ

Chaveirim va-chaveirot n'vareich.
Y'hi sheim Adonai m'vorach mei'atah v'ad olam.
N'vareich eloheinu she-achalnu mi-shello.
Baruch eloheinu she-achalnu mi-shello u-v'tuvo chayinu.
Baruch hu u-varuch sh'mo.

Siegmund Forst, 1959

We praise You, Eternal One, our God, Sovereign of the universe, whose goodness sustains the whole world. With grace, love and compassion You provide food for all Your creatures, for Your love is everlasting. Through Your great goodness we have never lacked our daily bread; may we always have sufficient, for Your great name's sake. Your goodness is the source of sustenance for all who live.

בָּרוּךְ אַתָּה יְיָ, אֱלֹהֵינוּ מֶלֶךְ הָעוֹלָם, הַזָּן אֶת הָעוֹלָם כֻּלּוֹ בְּטוּבוֹ בְּחֵן בְּחֶסֶד וּבְרַחֲמִים, הוּא נוֹתֵן לֶחֶם לְכָל בָּשָׂר כִּי לְעוֹלָם חַסְדּוֹ. וּבְטוּבוֹ הַגָּדוֹל תָּמִיד לֹא חָסַר לָנוּ, וְאַל יֶחְסַר לָנוּ מָזוֹן לְעוֹלָם וָעֶד. בַּעֲבוּר שְׁמוֹ הַגָּדוֹל, כִּי הוּא זָן וּמְפַרְנֵס לַכֹּל וּמֵטִיב לַכֹּל, וּמֵכִין מָזוֹן לְכָל בְּרִיּוֹתָיו אֲשֶׁר בָּרָא.

We praise You, O God, Provider of food for all.

בָּרוּךְ אַתָּה יְיָ, הַזָּן אֶת הַכֹּל.

Baruch atah Adonai eloheinu melech ha-olam ha-zan et ha-olam kullo b'tuvo b'chein b'chesed u-v'rachamim hu notein lechem l'chol basar ki l'olam chasdo u-v'tuvo ha-gadol tamid lo chasar lanu v'al yechsar lanu mazon l'olam va-ed ba'avur sh'mo ha-gadol ki hu zan u-m'farneis la-kol u-meitiv la-kol u-meichin mazon l'chol b'riyyotav asher bara. Baruch atah Adonai ha-zan et ha-kol.

We thank You, Eternal God, for the pleasant, good and spacious land You gave our ancestors; for leading us out of Egypt, and redeeming us from the house of bondage; for the covenant You have sealed into our hearts; for the Torah You have taught us, and the laws You have made known to us; for Your gracious gift of life and love; and for the food that sustains us day by day.

נוֹדֶה לְּךָ, יְיָ אֱלֹהֵינוּ, עַל שֶׁהִנְחַלְתָּ לַאֲבוֹתֵינוּ אֶרֶץ חֶמְדָּה טוֹבָה וּרְחָבָה, וְעַל שֶׁהוֹצֵאתָנוּ, יְיָ אֱלֹהֵינוּ, מֵאֶרֶץ מִצְרַיִם, וּפְדִיתָנוּ מִבֵּית עֲבָדִים, וְעַל בְּרִיתְךָ שֶׁחָתַמְתָּ בִּלְבָבֵנוּ, וְעַל תּוֹרָתְךָ שֶׁלִּמַּדְתָּנוּ, וְעַל חֻקֶּיךָ שֶׁהוֹדַעְתָּנוּ, וְעַל חַיִּים חֵן וָחֶסֶד שֶׁחוֹנַנְתָּנוּ, וְעַל אֲכִילַת מָזוֹן שָׁאַתָּה זָן וּמְפַרְנֵס אוֹתָנוּ תָּמִיד, בְּכָל יוֹם וּבְכָל עֵת וּבְכָל שָׁעָה.

Nodeh l'cha Adonai eloheinu al she-hinchalta la'avoteinu eretz chemdah tovah u-r'chavah v'al she-hotzeitanu Adonai eloheinu mei-eretz mitzrayim u-f'ditanu mi-beit avadim v'al b'rit'cha she-chatamta bi-l'vaveinu, v'al torat'cha she-limmad'tanu, v'al chukkecha she-hoda'tanu, v'al chayyim chein va-chesed she-chonantanu, v'al achilat mazon she-atah zan u-m'farneis otanu tamid b'chol yom u-v'chol eit u-v'chol sha'ah.

For all these things we thank and praise You. May Your name be praised continually by all who live, as it is written, 'When you have eaten and are satisfied, praise the Eternal One your God who has given you this good earth.' We praise You, O God for the earth and its sustenance.

וְעַל הַכֹּל, יְיָ אֱלֹהֵינוּ, אֲנַחְנוּ מוֹדִים לָךְ, וּמְבָרְכִים אוֹתָךְ, יִתְבָּרַךְ שִׁמְךָ בְּפִי כָּל חַי תָּמִיד לְעוֹלָם וָעֶד. כַּכָּתוּב, וְאָכַלְתָּ וְשָׂבָעְתָּ, וּבֵרַכְתָּ אֶת יְיָ אֱלֹהֶיךָ עַל הָאָרֶץ הַטֹּבָה אֲשֶׁר נָתַן לָךְ.

בָּרוּךְ אַתָּה יְיָ, עַל הָאָרֶץ וְעַל הַמָּזוֹן.

V'al ha-kol Adonai eloheinu anachnu modim lach u-m'varchim otach yitbarach shimcha b'fi chol chai tamid l'olam va-ed. Kakatuv v'achalta v'savata u-veirachta et Adonai elohecha al ha-aretz ha-tovah asher natan lach. Baruch atah Adonai al ha-aretz v'al ha-mazon.

On Shabbat:

Eternal God, strengthen our resolve to observe Your precepts, and especially the precept of the seventh day, the great and holy Sabbath, that we may lovingly rest on it and be refreshed by it, according to Your will.

רְצֵה וְהַחֲלִיצֵנוּ, יְיָ אֱלֹהֵינוּ, בְּמִצְוֹתֶיךָ וּבְמִצְוַת יוֹם הַשְּׁבִיעִי, הַשַּׁבָּת הַגָּדוֹל וְהַקָּדוֹשׁ הַזֶּה, לִשְׁבָּת בּוֹ וְלָנוּחַ בּוֹ בְּאַהֲבָה כְּמִצְוַת רְצוֹנֶךָ.

R'tzeh v'hachalitzeinu, Adonai eloheinu, b'mitzvotecha u-v'mitzvat yom ha-sh'vi'i, ha-shabbat ha-gaddol v'ha-kadosh ha-zeh, lishbot bo v'lanu'ach bo b'ahavah k'mitzvat r'tzonecha.

Have compassion, Eternal God, on Your people Israel and all the inhabitants of Your world. Guide and sustain us, grant us prosperity and liberty, and may we soon be freed from all our troubles. Let us not be in need of gifts or loans, but dependent only on Your generous providence, so that we may never be embarrassed or put to shame.

רַחֵם, יְיָ אֱלֹהֵינוּ, עַל יִשְׂרָאֵל עַמֶּךָ, וְעַל כָּל־יוֹשְׁבֵי תֵבֵל אַרְצֶךָ. אֱלֹהֵינוּ, אָבִינוּ, רְעֵנוּ, זוּנֵנוּ, פַּרְנְסֵנוּ, וְכַלְכְּלֵנוּ, וְהַרְוִיחֵנוּ, וְהַרְוַח לָנוּ יְיָ אֱלֹהֵינוּ מְהֵרָה מִכָּל צָרוֹתֵינוּ, וְנָא אַל תַּצְרִיכֵנוּ, יְיָ אֱלֹהֵינוּ, לֹא לִידֵי מַתְּנַת בָּשָׂר וָדָם, וְלֹא לִידֵי הַלְוָאָתָם, כִּי אִם לְיָדְךָ הַמְּלֵאָה, הַפְּתוּחָה, הַקְּדוֹשָׁה וְהָרְחָבָה, שֶׁלֹּא נֵבוֹשׁ וְלֹא נִכָּלֵם לְעוֹלָם וָעֶד.

Racheim Adonai eloheinu al Yisra'eil ammecha, v'al kol yoshvei teiveil artzecha. Eloheinu avinu r'einu zuneinu farn'seinu v'chalk'leinu v'harvicheinu v'harvach lanu Adonai eloheinu m'heirah mi-kol tzaroteinu, v'na al tatzricheinu Adonai eloheinu lo liydei matnat basar va-dam v'lo liydei ha-l'va'atam ki im l'yad'cha ha-m'lei'ah ha-p'tuchah ha-k'doshah v'ha-r'chavah she-lo neivosh v'lo nikkaleim l'olam va-ed.

Our God and God of our ancestors, be mindful of us and all Your people of the House of Israel. Grant us well-being and blessing, life and peace, on this Festival of Unleavened bread.
Remember us this day for well-being. Amen.
Bless us this day with Your presence. Amen.
Grant us this day continued life. Amen.

אֱלֹהֵינוּ וֵאלֹהֵי אֲבוֹתֵינוּ, יַעֲלֶה וְיָבֹא,
וְיִזָּכֵר זִכְרוֹנֵנוּ וּפִקְדוֹנֵנוּ, וְזִכְרוֹן כָּל עַמְּךָ
בֵּית יִשְׂרָאֵל לְפָנֶיךָ, לִפְלֵיטָה, לְטוֹבָה,
לְחֵן וּלְחֶסֶד וּלְרַחֲמִים, לְחַיִּים וּלְשָׁלוֹם,
בְּיוֹם חַג הַמַּצּוֹת הַזֶּה.
זָכְרֵנוּ, יְיָ אֱלֹהֵינוּ, בּוֹ לְטוֹבָה. אָמֵן.
וּפָקְדֵנוּ בוֹ לִבְרָכָה. אָמֵן.
וְהוֹשִׁיעֵנוּ בוֹ לְחַיִּים. אָמֵן.

Eloheinu v'eilohei avoteinu ya'aleh v'yizacheir zichroneinu u-fikdoneinu v'zichron kol am'cha beit Yisra'el l'fanecha li-f'leitah l'tovah l'chein l'chesed u-l'rachamim l'chayim u-l'shalom b'yom chag ha-matzot ha-zeh. Zochreinu Adonai eloheinu bo l'tovah. Amen U-fokdeinu vo li-v'rachah. Amen. v'hoshiyeinu vo l'chayyim. Amen.

And let the vision of Jerusalem, the holy city, be fulfilled in our time.
We praise You, compassionate God, Builder of Jerusalem. Amen.

וּבְנֵה יְרוּשָׁלַיִם עִיר הַקֹּדֶשׁ בִּמְהֵרָה
בְיָמֵינוּ. בָּרוּךְ אַתָּה יְיָ, בּוֹנֵה בְרַחֲמָיו
יְרוּשָׁלָיִם. אָמֵן.

U-v'neih y'rushalayim ir ha-kodesh bimheirah v'yameinu. Baruch atah Adonai boneih v'rachamav y'rushalayim. Amen.

We praise You, Eternal God, Sovereign of the universe, our Creator and Redeemer, the Holy One of Jacob and the Shepherd of Israel, good and beneficent to all. You have shown us love and kindness always; day by day You grant us grace and compassion, deliverance and freedom, prosperity and blessing, life and peace.
May we never lack what we need for our good.

בָּרוּךְ אַתָּה יְיָ אֱלֹהֵינוּ מֶלֶךְ הָעוֹלָם,
הָאֵל, אָבִינוּ, מַלְכֵּנוּ, אַדִּירֵנוּ, בּוֹרְאֵנוּ,
גּוֹאֲלֵנוּ, יוֹצְרֵנוּ, קְדוֹשֵׁנוּ קְדוֹשׁ יַעֲקֹב,
רוֹעֵנוּ רוֹעֵה יִשְׂרָאֵל, הַמֶּלֶךְ הַטּוֹב
וְהַמֵּטִיב לַכֹּל, שֶׁבְּכָל יוֹם וָיוֹם הוּא
הֵטִיב, הוּא מֵטִיב, הוּא יֵיטִיב לָנוּ. הוּא
גְמָלָנוּ, הוּא גוֹמְלֵנוּ, הוּא יִגְמְלֵנוּ לָעַד,
לְחֵן וּלְחֶסֶד וּלְרַחֲמִים וּלְרֶוַח הַצָּלָה
וְהַצְלָחָה, בְּרָכָה וִישׁוּעָה, נֶחָמָה,
פַּרְנָסָה וְכַלְכָּלָה, וְרַחֲמִים וְחַיִּים וְשָׁלוֹם
וְכָל טוֹב, וּמִכָּל טוּב אַל יְחַסְּרֵנוּ.

Baruch atah Adonai eloheinu melech ha-olam ha-eil avinu malkeinu addireinu bor'einu go'aleinu yotzreinu k'dosheinu k'dosh Ya'akov. Ro'einu ro'eih Yisra'el ha-melech ha-tov v'ha-meitiv la-kol she-b'chol yom va-yom. Hu heitiv hu meitiv hu yeitiv lanu hu g'malanu hu gomleinu hu yigm'leinu la'ad, l'chein u-l'chesed u-l'rachamim u-l'revach ha-tzalah v'hatzlachah b'rachah vishu'ah nechamah parnasah v'chalkalah, v'rachamim v'chayyim v'shalom v'chol tov u-mi-kol tov al y'chassreinu.

הָרַחֲמָן, הוּא יִמְלוֹךְ עָלֵינוּ לְעוֹלָם וָעֶד.
הָרַחֲמָן, הוּא יִתְבָּרַךְ בַּשָּׁמַיִם וּבָאָרֶץ.
הָרַחֲמָן, הוּא יִשְׁתַּבַּח לְדוֹר דּוֹרִים, וְיִתְפָּאַר בָּנוּ לָנֶצַח נְצָחִים, וְיִתְהַדַּר בָּנוּ לָעַד וּלְעוֹלְמֵי עוֹלָמִים.
הָרַחֲמָן, הוּא יִשְׁלַח בְּרָכָה מְרֻבָּה בַּבַּיִת הַזֶּה, וְעַל שֻׁלְחָן זֶה שֶׁאָכַלְנוּ עָלָיו.
הָרַחֲמָן, הוּא יִשְׁלַח לָנוּ אֶת אֵלִיָּהוּ הַנָּבִיא זָכוּר לַטּוֹב, וִיבַשֶּׂר לָנוּ בְּשׂוֹרוֹת טוֹבוֹת יְשׁוּעוֹת וְנֶחָמוֹת.
הָרַחֲמָן, הוּא יְבָרֵךְ אוֹתָנוּ וְאֶת כָּל אֲשֶׁר לָנוּ, כְּמוֹ שֶׁנִּתְבָּרְכוּ אֲבוֹתֵינוּ, אַבְרָהָם יִצְחָק וְיַעֲקֹב, וְאִמּוֹתֵינוּ שָׂרָה רִבְקָה רָחֵל וְלֵאָה בַּכֹּל, מִכֹּל, כֹּל, כֵּן יְבָרֵךְ אוֹתָנוּ כֻּלָּנוּ יַחַד בִּבְרָכָה שְׁלֵמָה, וְנֹאמַר אָמֵן.

May the Merciful One rule over us for ever.
May the Merciful One be praised in heaven and on earth.
May the Merciful One be praised by every generation, extolled and glorified by us for ever.
May the Merciful One bless this house, and this table at which we have eaten.
May the Merciful One send us Elijah the Prophet with good tidings of deliverance and consolation.
Merciful One, bless us and all our dear ones. As you blessed our ancestors Abraham, Isaac and Jacob; Sarah, Rebekah, Rachel and Leah; in every way, so bless us, one and all. And let us say: Amen.

(בְּשַׁבָּת: הָרַחֲמָן, הוּא יַנְחִילֵנוּ יוֹם שֶׁכֻּלּוֹ שַׁבָּת וּמְנוּחָה לְחַיֵּי הָעוֹלָמִים.)

(On Shabbat:
May the Merciful One grant us perfect Shabbat rest and peace in the life of eternity.)

הָרַחֲמָן, הוּא יַנְחִילֵנוּ יוֹם שֶׁכֻּלּוֹ טוֹב.

הָרַחֲמָן, הוּא יְזַכֵּנוּ לִימוֹת הַגְּאֻלָּה וּלְחַיֵּי הָעוֹלָם הַבָּא.

May the Merciful One permit us to see a time that is all good.
May the Merciful One make us worthy to witness the time of redemption.

Ha-rachaman hu yimloch aleinu l'olam va-ed.
Ha-rachaman hu yitbarach ba-shamayim u-va-aretz.
Ha-rachaman hu yishtabbach l'dor dorim v'yitpa'ar banu l'neitzach n'tzachim v'yithaddar banu la'ad u-l'olmei olamim.
Ha-rachaman hu yishlach b'rachah m'rubbah ba-bayit ha-zeh v'al shulchan zeh she-achalnu alav.
Ha-rachaman hu yishlach lanu et Eliyahu ha-navi zachur la-tov viyvaseir lanu b'sorot tovot y'shu'ot v'nechamot.
Ha-rachaman hu y'vareich otanu v'et kol asher lanu k'mo she-nitbar'chu avoteinu Avraham, Yitzchak v'Ya'akov, v'imoteinu Sarah, Rivkah, Rachel v'Le'ah ba-kol mi-kol kol, kein y'vareich otanu kulanu yachad bi-v'rachah sh'leimah v'nomar Amen.
(Ha-rachaman hu yanchileinu yom she-kullo shabbat u-m'nuchah l'chayyei ha-olamim.)
Ha-rachaman hu yanchileinu yom she-kullo tov.
Ha-rachaman hu y'zakkeinu liymot ha-g'ullah u-l'chayyei ha-olam ha-ba.

Thanksgiving for the Meal

Continue here

We have eaten and been satisfied. Help us to be responsive to the needs of others and to listen to their cry for food. Open our eyes and our hearts, so that we may share Your gifts, and help to remove hunger and want from our world.

May the Most High, Source of perfect peace, grant peace to us, to all Israel, and to all humanity.

עֹשֶׂה שָׁלוֹם בִּמְרוֹמָיו, הוּא יַעֲשֶׂה שָׁלוֹם עָלֵינוּ וְעַל כָּל יִשְׂרָאֵל, וְעַל כָּל־בְּנֵי־אָדָם.

Oseh shalom bi-m'romav hu ya'aseh shalom aleinu v'al kol Yisra'el v'al kol b'nei adam.

Eternal God, grant strength to Your people. Eternal God, bless Your people with peace.

יְיָ עֹז לְעַמּוֹ יִתֵּן,
יְיָ יְבָרֵךְ אֶת עַמּוֹ בַשָּׁלוֹם.

Adonai oz l'ammo yitein Adonai y'vareich et ammo va-shalom.

The third glass כּוֹס שֶׁל בְּרָכָה

We raise our glasses in acknowledgement of the third of God's promises:

I will redeem you with an outstretched arm and with great acts of judgement.

"**וְגָאַלְתִּי** אֶתְכֶם בִּזְרוֹעַ נְטוּיָה וּבִשְׁפָטִים גְּדֹלִים."

We praise You, Eternal One our God, Sovereign of the universe, Creator of the fruit of the vine.

בָּרוּךְ אַתָּה יְיָ אֱלֹהֵינוּ מֶלֶךְ הָעוֹלָם, בּוֹרֵא פְּרִי הַגָּפֶן.

Baruch atah Adonai eloheinu melech ha-olam borei p'ri ha-gafen.

Lean to the left and drink the third glass of wine

Fill the fourth glass of wine
(and those of Elijah and Miriam, if this has not already been done)

God's wrath – or God's love?

This is the point of the *Seder* at which we begin to look to the future and remind ourselves that this festival is concerned not only with an account of past oppression and redemption, but also with the future of humanity.

Before doing that, the traditional *Haggadah*, which was often read in times of great oppression and danger, acknowledged the persecutions of the past with these harsh and bitter words:

Pour out Your wrath on the nations that do not know You and upon the kingdoms that do not invoke Your name for they have devoured Jacob and destroyed his home. (Psalm 79:6-7)

שְׁפֹךְ חֲמָתְךָ אֶל־הַגּוֹיִם אֲשֶׁר לֹא־יְדָעוּךָ
וְעַל מַמְלָכוֹת אֲשֶׁר בְּשִׁמְךָ לֹא קָרָאוּ.
כִּי־אָכַל אֶת־יַעֲקֹב וְאֶת־נָוֵהוּ הֵשַׁמּוּ.

But throughout the ages there were those who protected the Jews and respected their customs and traditions. The following passage recognises that, in our day, we acknowledge the goodwill of so many towards us, and this is our Passover prayer for the future:

Pour out Your love on the nations who have known You and on the kingdoms who call upon Your name. For they have shown kindness to the descendants of Jacob and protected the people of Israel from their persecutors. May their reward be to see Israel at peace, and may they share in the joy of all Your nations.

שְׁפֹךְ אַהֲבָתְךָ אֶל־הַגּוֹיִם אֲשֶׁר יְדָעוּךָ
וְעַל מַמְלָכוֹת אֲשֶׁר בְּשִׁמְךָ קוֹרְאִים.
בִּגְלַל חֲסָדִים שֶׁהֵם עוֹשִׂים עִם זֶרַע
יַעֲקֹב וּמְגִנִּים עַל עַמְּךָ יִשְׂרָאֵל מִפְּנֵי
אוֹכְלֵיהֶם. יִזְכּוּ לִרְאוֹת בְּסֻכַּת בְּחִירֶיךָ
וְלִשְׂמֹחַ בְּשִׂמְחַת גּוֹיֶיךָ.

Ben Shahn, Weeping Man

Hallel הַלֵּל

Psalm 117

Praise the Eternal One, all you nations! Extol God, all you peoples! For great is God's love for us; God's faithfulness endures for ever. Halleluyah!

הַלְלוּ אֶת־יְהֹוָה כָּל־גּוֹיִם שַׁבְּחוּהוּ
כָּל־הָאֻמִּים. כִּי גָבַר עָלֵינוּ חַסְדּוֹ
וֶאֱמֶת־יְהֹוָה לְעוֹלָם –
הַלְלוּיָהּ!

Hallelu et Adonai kol goyim shabb'chu'hu kol ha-ummim
Ki gavar aleinu chasdo ve-emet Adonai l'olam – Halleluyah!

Psalm 118

Give thanks to the Eternal One, who is good
whose love endures for ever.
Let Israel declare:
God's love endures for ever.
Let the House of Aaron declare:
God's love endures for ever.
Let all God-fearing people declare:
God's love endures for ever.

הוֹדוּ לַיהֹוָה כִּי־טוֹב
כִּי לְעוֹלָם חַסְדּוֹ.
יֹאמַר־נָא יִשְׂרָאֵל
כִּי לְעוֹלָם חַסְדּוֹ.
יֹאמְרוּ נָא בֵית־אַהֲרֹן
כִּי לְעוֹלָם חַסְדּוֹ.
יֹאמְרוּ נָא יִרְאֵי יְהֹוָה
כִּי לְעוֹלָם חַסְדּוֹ.

Hodu l'Adonai ki tov – ki l'olam chasdo! Yomar na Yisra'el – ki l'olam chasdo,
Yomru na veit Aharon – ki l'olam chasdo, Yomru na yir'ei Adonai – ki l'olam chasdo.

In my distress I called out to God
Who answered me and set me free.
God is with me, I am not afraid
What can mere mortals do to me?
With God as my helper
I can face any foe.
It is better to take refuge in God than
to rely on human beings.
It is better to take refuge in God than
to rely on those in power.
God is my strength and my shield
and has become my salvation.
Hear! Glad songs of triumph in the tents
of the righteous!
The Eternal One does mighty deeds
I shall not die but live
to tell of God's deeds.

מִן־הַמֵּצַר קָרָאתִי יָּהּ עָנָנִי בַמֶּרְחָב יָהּ.
יְהֹוָה לִי לֹא אִירָא מַה־יַּעֲשֶׂה לִי אָדָם.
יְהֹוָה לִי בְּעֹזְרָי וַאֲנִי אֶרְאֶה בְשֹׂנְאָי.
טוֹב לַחֲסוֹת בַּיהֹוָה מִבְּטֹחַ בָּאָדָם.
טוֹב לַחֲסוֹת בַּיהֹוָה מִבְּטֹחַ בִּנְדִיבִים.
עָזִּי וְזִמְרָת יָהּ וַיְהִי־לִי לִישׁוּעָה.
קוֹל רִנָּה וִישׁוּעָה בְּאָהֳלֵי צַדִּיקִים
יְמִין יְהֹוָה עֹשָׂה חָיִל.
יְמִין יְהֹוָה רוֹמֵמָה
יְמִין יְהֹוָה עֹשָׂה חָיִל.
לֹא אָמוּת כִּי־אֶחְיֶה
וַאֲסַפֵּר מַעֲשֵׂי יָהּ.

Open for me the gates of righteousness,
let me enter them and give thanks to God.
This is the gate of the Eternal One,
the righteous shall enter it.

פִּתְחוּ־לִי שַׁעֲרֵי־צֶדֶק
אָבֹא־בָם אוֹדֶה יָהּ.
זֶה־הַשַּׁעַר לַיהוָה
צַדִּיקִים יָבֹאוּ בוֹ.

I thank You for You have answered me
and become my salvation.
The stone that the builders rejected
has become the chief cornerstone.
This is the work of the Eternal One,
it is marvellous in our sight.
This is the day that God has made,
let us rejoice and be glad in it.

אוֹדְךָ כִּי עֲנִיתָנִי וַתְּהִי־לִי לִישׁוּעָה.
אֶבֶן מָאֲסוּ הַבּוֹנִים הָיְתָה לְרֹאשׁ פִּנָּה.
מֵאֵת יְהוָה הָיְתָה זֹּאת הִיא נִפְלָאת
בְּעֵינֵינוּ.
זֶה־הַיּוֹם עָשָׂה יְהוָה
נָגִילָה וְנִשְׂמְחָה בוֹ.

Eternal God, deliver us!
Eternal God, prosper us!

אָנָּא יְהוָה הוֹשִׁיעָה נָּא!
אָנָּא יְהוָה הַצְלִיחָה נָּא!

Blessed are you who come in God's name,
here, in God's house, may you be blessed.
You are my God and I thank You,
You are my God and I exalt You.

בָּרוּךְ הַבָּא בְּשֵׁם יְהוָה,
בֵּרַכְנוּכֶם מִבֵּית יְהוָה.
אֵלִי אַתָּה וְאוֹדֶךָּ
אֱלֹהַי אֲרוֹמְמֶךָּ.

Give thanks to the Eternal One
who is good,
whose love endures for ever.

הוֹדוּ לַיהוָה כִּי־טוֹב
כִּי לְעוֹלָם חַסְדּוֹ.

Pitchu li sha'arei tzedek avo vam odeh Yah.
Zeh ha-sha'ar l'Adonai tzaddikim yavo'u vo.
Od'cha ki anitani va-t'hi li liyshu'ah.
Even ma'asu ha-bonim hay'tah l'rosh pinnah.
Mei'eit Adonai hay'tah zot hi niflat b'eineinu.
Zeh ha-yom asah Adonai nagilah v'nism'chah vo.
Anna Adonai hoshi'ah na. Anna Adonai hatzlichah na.
Baruch ha-ba b'sheim Adonai beirachnuchem mi-beit Adonai.
Eili atah v'odeka, elohai arom'meka.
Hodu l'Adonai ki tov, ki l'olam chasdo.

Birkat ha-shir בִּרְכַּת הַשִּׁיר

One or more of the following three songs of praise may be omitted

From Psalm 136

Give thanks to the Eternal One who is good:
  God's love endures for ever.
Give thanks to the God above all gods:
  God's love endures for ever.
Give thanks to the Power above all powers:
  God's love endures for ever.
To the One who alone performs great wonders:
  Whose love endures for ever.
Who in wisdom made the heavens:
  God's love endures for ever.
Who spread forth the earth above the waters:
  God's love endures for ever.
Who created the great lights:
  God's love endures for ever.
The sun to rule by day:
  God's love endures for ever.
The moon and stars to rule by night:
  God's love endures for ever.
Who brought Israel out of Egypt:
  God's love endures for ever.
With mighty hand and outstretched arm:
  God's love endures for ever.
Who divided the Sea of Reeds in two:
  God's love endures for ever.
And enabled Israel to pass through it:
  God's love endures for ever.
And led the people through the wilderness:
  God's love endures for ever.
Who remembered us in our deep distress:
  God's love endures for ever.
And delivered us from our enemies:
  God's love endures for ever.
Who gives food for all creatures:
  God's love endures for ever.
O give thanks to the God of heaven:
  God's love endures for ever.

הוֹדוּ לַיהוָה כִּי־טוֹב
כִּי לְעוֹלָם חַסְדּוֹ׃
הוֹדוּ לֵאלֹהֵי הָאֱלֹהִים
כִּי לְעוֹלָם חַסְדּוֹ׃
הוֹדוּ לַאֲדֹנֵי הָאֲדֹנִים
כִּי לְעוֹלָם חַסְדּוֹ׃
לְעֹשֵׂה נִפְלָאוֹת גְּדֹלוֹת לְבַדּוֹ
כִּי לְעוֹלָם חַסְדּוֹ׃
לְעֹשֵׂה הַשָּׁמַיִם בִּתְבוּנָה
כִּי לְעוֹלָם חַסְדּוֹ׃
לְרֹקַע הָאָרֶץ עַל־הַמָּיִם
כִּי לְעוֹלָם חַסְדּוֹ׃
לְעֹשֵׂה אוֹרִים גְּדֹלִים
כִּי לְעוֹלָם חַסְדּוֹ׃
אֶת־הַשֶּׁמֶשׁ לְמֶמְשֶׁלֶת בַּיּוֹם
כִּי לְעוֹלָם חַסְדּוֹ׃
אֶת־הַיָּרֵחַ וְכוֹכָבִים לְמֶמְשְׁלוֹת בַּלָּיְלָה
כִּי לְעוֹלָם חַסְדּוֹ׃
וַיּוֹצֵא יִשְׂרָאֵל מִתּוֹכָם
כִּי לְעוֹלָם חַסְדּוֹ׃
בְּיָד חֲזָקָה וּבִזְרוֹעַ נְטוּיָה
כִּי לְעוֹלָם חַסְדּוֹ׃
לְגֹזֵר יַם־סוּף לִגְזָרִים
כִּי לְעוֹלָם חַסְדּוֹ׃
וְהֶעֱבִיר יִשְׂרָאֵל בְּתוֹכוֹ
כִּי לְעוֹלָם חַסְדּוֹ׃
לְמוֹלִיךְ עַמּוֹ בַּמִּדְבָּר
כִּי לְעוֹלָם חַסְדּוֹ׃
שֶׁבְּשִׁפְלֵנוּ זָכַר־לָנוּ
כִּי לְעוֹלָם חַסְדּוֹ׃
וַיִּפְרְקֵנוּ מִצָּרֵינוּ
כִּי לְעוֹלָם חַסְדּוֹ׃
נֹתֵן לֶחֶם לְכָל־בָּשָׂר
כִּי לְעוֹלָם חַסְדּוֹ׃
הוֹדוּ לְאֵל הַשָּׁמָיִם
כִּי לעולם חסדו׃

Blessing of Song

Nishmat

נִשְׁמַת

Let all the living give praise to Your name, our Eternal God. Let every human spirit acclaim Your majesty for ever. Through all eternity You are God; we have no Ruler but You, no other Helper or Redeemer to sustain and pity us in time of trouble and distress.

נִשְׁמַת כָּל חַי, תְּבָרֵךְ אֶת שִׁמְךָ יְיָ אֱלֹהֵינוּ, וְרוּחַ כָּל בָּשָׂר תְּפָאֵר וּתְרוֹמֵם זִכְרְךָ מַלְכֵּנוּ תָּמִיד, מִן הָעוֹלָם וְעַד הָעוֹלָם אַתָּה אֵל, וּמִבַּלְעָדֶיךָ אֵין לָנוּ מֶלֶךְ גּוֹאֵל וּמוֹשִׁיעַ, פּוֹדֶה וּמַצִּיל וּמְפַרְנֵס וּמְרַחֵם בְּכָל עֵת צָרָה וְצוּקָה, אֵין לָנוּ מֶלֶךְ אֶלָּא אָתָּה.

From Egypt until now You redeemed us, Eternal God, and from the house of bondage You released us. In times of famine You have sustained us. From the sword You have delivered us, from plagues and diseases rescued us.

מִמִּצְרַיִם גְּאַלְתָּנוּ, יְיָ אֱלֹהֵינוּ, וּמִבֵּית עֲבָדִים פְּדִיתָנוּ. בְּרָעָב זַנְתָּנוּ, וּבְשָׂבָע כִּלְכַּלְתָּנוּ, מֵחֶרֶב הִצַּלְתָּנוּ, וּמִדֶּבֶר מִלַּטְתָּנוּ, וּמֵחֳלָיִם רָעִים וְנֶאֱמָנִים דִּלִּיתָנוּ.

Until this day, Your mercy has upheld us, Your love has never failed us. Do not forsake us, Eternal God: remain our help forever.

עַד הֵנָּה עֲזָרוּנוּ רַחֲמֶיךָ, וְלֹא עֲזָבוּנוּ חֲסָדֶיךָ, וְאַל תִּטְּשֵׁנוּ, יְיָ אֱלֹהֵינוּ, לָנֶצַח.

Therefore we praise You, proclaim Your glory and bless Your holy name, as it is said: 'Bless the Eternal One my soul; let all that is within me bless God's holy name.'

נְהַלֶּלְךָ וּנְשַׁבֵּחֲךָ וּנְפָאֶרְךָ, וּנְבָרֵךְ אֶת שֵׁם קָדְשֶׁךָ, כָּאָמוּר, לְדָוִד, בָּרְכִי נַפְשִׁי אֶת יְיָ, וְכָל קְרָבַי אֶת שֵׁם קָדְשׁוֹ.

Yishtabbach

יִשְׁתַּבַּח

O great and holy God and Ruler, Your name be praised for ever more in heaven and on earth. To You, our God and God of our ancestors, let hymns and psalms be sung unceasingly. All might and majesty, all victory and greatness, all glory, holiness and sovereignty are Yours. To You all thanks are due, all praise belongs, from now until the end of time.

יִשְׁתַּבַּח שִׁמְךָ לָעַד מַלְכֵּנוּ, הָאֵל הַמֶּלֶךְ הַגָּדוֹל וְהַקָּדוֹשׁ בַּשָּׁמַיִם וּבָאָרֶץ. כִּי לְךָ נָאֶה, יְיָ אֱלֹהֵינוּ וֵאלֹהֵי אֲבוֹתֵינוּ, שִׁיר וּשְׁבָחָה, הַלֵּל וְזִמְרָה, עֹז וּמֶמְשָׁלָה, נֶצַח, גְּדֻלָּה וּגְבוּרָה, תְּהִלָּה וְתִפְאֶרֶת, קְדֻשָּׁה וּמַלְכוּת. בְּרָכוֹת וְהוֹדָאוֹת מֵעַתָּה וְעַד עוֹלָם.

We praise You, our Eternal God and Ruler: may our songs of praise, gratitude and reverence be acceptable to You, Author of wonders, Source of the life of all worlds.

בָּרוּךְ אַתָּה יְיָ, אֵל מֶלֶךְ גָּדוֹל בַּתִּשְׁבָּחוֹת, אֵל הַהוֹדָאוֹת, אֲדוֹן הַנִּפְלָאוֹת, הַבּוֹחֵר בְּשִׁירֵי זִמְרָה, מֶלֶךְ, אֵל, חֵי הָעוֹלָמִים.

The fourth glass כּוֹס רְבִיעִי

We raise our glasses in acknowledgement of the fourth of God's promises:

I will take you to be My people and I will be your God.

"**וְלָקַחְתִּי** אֶתְכֶם לִי לְעָם וְהָיִיתִי לָכֶם לֵאלֹהִים."

Praised are You, Eternal One our God, Creator of the fruit of the vine.

בָּרוּךְ אַתָּה יְיָ אֱלֹהֵינוּ מֶלֶךְ הָעוֹלָם, בּוֹרֵא פְּרִי הַגָּפֶן.

Baruch atah Adonai eloheinu melech ha-olam borei p'ri ha-gafen.

Lean to the left and drink the fourth glass of wine

The counting of the *Omer*

The following may be read when a *Seder* is held on the second night of *Pesach*

The second day of *Pesach* sees the beginning of the counting of the *Omer*, a seven-week period that will conclude with the festival of *Shavu'ot*. It is regarded by the rabbis as representing the time it took our ancestors to journey from Egypt to Mount Sinai, where they received the Ten Commandments.

Let this journey of our ancestors from the fetters of slavery, through a wilderness of uncertainty, to a place where they found guidance in God's teaching symbolise a similar journey for us: may we too learn the lessons of this *Seder*: to strive for the knowledge and understanding to liberate ourselves from whatever holds us enslaved.

We praise You, Eternal God, Sovereign of the universe: You sanctify us by Your commandments and enjoin us to count the days of the *Omer*.

בָּרוּךְ אַתָּה יְיָ אֱלֹהֵינוּ מֶלֶךְ הָעוֹלָם, אֲשֶׁר קִדְּשָׁנוּ בְּמִצְוֹתָיו, וְצִוָּנוּ עַל סְפִירַת הָעוֹמֶר.

Baruch atah Adonai eloheinu melech ha-olam asher kidd'shanu b'mitzvotav v'tzivvanu al s'firat ha-omer.

Today is the first day of the *Omer*.

Ha-yom yom echad la-omer.

הַיּוֹם יוֹם אֶחָד לָעוֹמֶר.

Miriam's cup

Elijah's cup

The door is opened

The custom of filling a cup with water to represent the contribution of Miriam to the story of our people is a creative innovation of progressive Judaism. But as we have read:

וַתָּמָת שָׁם מִרְיָם וַתִּקָּבֵר שָׁם. וְלֹא־הָיָה מַיִם לָעֵדָה...

And Miriam died there and there was no water for the community...

Not to acknowledge the role of Miriam in the history of our ancestors' escape from Egypt is to fail to tell the full story. Miriam's Well sustained the people in the wilderness; may this cup of water remind us of the role she played in our deliverance from Egypt.

We fill the cup with water for Miriam to give thanks for our deliverance and place it alongside that of Elijah to emphasise the task with which we are all charged.

The sages of old could not decide whether to drink a fifth cup at the *Seder*, for there is a fifth promise in the Torah:

וְהֵבֵאתִי אֶתְכֶם אֶל־הָאָרֶץ אֲשֶׁר נָשָׂאתִי אֶת־יָדִי לָתֵת אֹתָהּ לְאַבְרָהָם לְיִצְחָק וּלְיַעֲקֹב...

And I will bring you to the land which I promised to give to your ancestors, to Abraham, Isaac and Jacob...

In the end, the rabbis decided that only Elijah could answer the question of whether or not a fifth cup should be drunk. According to tradition, the arrival of this prophet would herald the Messianic Age and lead to all unsolved questions being answered.

We fill the cup with wine for Elijah to anticipate the joy of the Messianic Age but we do not drink it, for we live in an age that is not yet redeemed.

As we open the door to welcome Elijah, we seek to understand the message of our past, and our duty to the present. We too can play our part in sustaining and nurturing our faith and our hope, as it is said:

Behold, I will send you Elijah the prophet before the coming of the great and awesome day of the Eternal One.

He will turn the hearts of parents to their children, and the hearts of children to their parents.

And then it shall come to pass that your sons and daughters shall prophesy,

The old shall dream dreams, and the young shall see visions.

They shall beat their swords into ploughshares and their spears into pruning hooks.

Nation shall not lift up sword against nation, and never again shall they learn to make war.

Then everyone shall sit under their vines and under their fig trees, and none shall make them afraid.

Speedily, in our days. Amen.

בִּמְהֵרָה בְיָמֵינוּ. אָמֵן.

Bim'heirah v'yameinu. Amen.

The door is closed

The *Seder* can continue with a number of songs. The *Seder* concludes on page 50.

כִּי לוֹ נָאֶה

כִּי לוֹ נָאֶה, כִּי לוֹ יָאֶה.

אַדִּיר בִּמְלוּכָה, בָּחוּר כַּהֲלָכָה, גְּדוּדָיו יֹאמְרוּ לוֹ:
לְךָ וּלְךָ, לְךָ כִּי לְךָ, לְךָ אַף לְךָ, לְךָ יְיָ הַמַּמְלָכָה. כִּי לוֹ נָאֶה, כִּי לוֹ יָאֶה.

דָּגוּל בִּמְלוּכָה, הָדוּר כַּהֲלָכָה, וָתִיקָיו יֹאמְרוּ לוֹ:
לְךָ וּלְךָ, לְךָ כִּי לְךָ, לְךָ אַף לְךָ, לְךָ יְיָ הַמַּמְלָכָה. כִּי לוֹ נָאֶה, כִּי לוֹ יָאֶה.

זַכַּאי בִּמְלוּכָה, חָסִין כַּהֲלָכָה, טַפְסְרָיו יֹאמְרוּ לוֹ:
לְךָ וּלְךָ, לְךָ כִּי לְךָ, לְךָ אַף לְךָ, לְךָ יְיָ הַמַּמְלָכָה. כִּי לוֹ נָאֶה, כִּי לוֹ יָאֶה.

יָחִיד בִּמְלוּכָה, כַּבִּיר כַּהֲלָכָה, לִמּוּדָיו יֹאמְרוּ לוֹ:
לְךָ וּלְךָ, לְךָ כִּי לְךָ, לְךָ אַף לְךָ, לְךָ יְיָ הַמַּמְלָכָה. כִּי לוֹ נָאֶה, כִּי לוֹ יָאֶה.

מוֹשֵׁל בִּמְלוּכָה, נוֹרָא כַּהֲלָכָה, סְבִיבָיו יֹאמְרוּ לוֹ:
לְךָ וּלְךָ, לְךָ כִּי לְךָ, לְךָ אַף לְךָ, לְךָ יְיָ הַמַּמְלָכָה. כִּי לוֹ נָאֶה, כִּי לוֹ יָאֶה.

עָנָו בִּמְלוּכָה, פּוֹדֶה כַּהֲלָכָה, צַדִּיקָיו יֹאמְרוּ לוֹ:
לְךָ וּלְךָ, לְךָ כִּי לְךָ, לְךָ אַף לְךָ, לְךָ יְיָ הַמַּמְלָכָה. כִּי לוֹ נָאֶה, כִּי לוֹ יָאֶה.

קָדוֹשׁ בִּמְלוּכָה, רַחוּם כַּהֲלָכָה, שִׁנְאַנָּיו יֹאמְרוּ לוֹ:
לְךָ וּלְךָ, לְךָ כִּי לְךָ, לְךָ אַף לְךָ, לְךָ יְיָ הַמַּמְלָכָה. כִּי לוֹ נָאֶה, כִּי לוֹ יָאֶה.

תַּקִּיף בִּמְלוּכָה, תּוֹמֵךְ כַּהֲלָכָה, תְּמִימָיו יֹאמְרוּ לוֹ:
לְךָ וּלְךָ, לְךָ כִּי לְךָ, לְךָ אַף לְךָ, לְךָ יְיָ הַמַּמְלָכָה. כִּי לוֹ נָאֶה, כִּי לוֹ יָאֶה.

Paul Solomons, 2010

Ki lo na'eh

Ki lo na'eh, ki lo ya'eh

Addir bi-m'luchah, bachur ka-halachah, g'dudav yom'ru lo. L'cha u-l'cha l'cha ki l'cha, l'cha af l'cha, l'cha Adonai ha-mamlachah, ki lo na'eh, ki lo ya'eh.

Dagul bi-m'luchah, hadur ka-halachah, vatikav yom'ru lo. L'cha u-l'cha l'cha ki l'cha, l'cha af l'cha, l'cha Adonai ha-mamlachah, ki lo na'eh, ki lo ya'eh.

Zakkai bi-m'luchah, chasin ka-halachah, tafs'rav yom'ru lo. L'cha u-l'cha l'cha ki l'cha, l'cha af l'cha, l'cha Adonai ha-mamlachah, ki lo na'eh, ki lo ya'eh.

Yachid bi-m'luchah, kabbir ka-halachah, limmudav yom'ru lo. L'cha u-l'cha l'cha ki l'cha, l'cha af l'cha, l'cha Adonai ha-mamlachah, ki lo na'eh, ki lo ya'eh.

Mosheil bi-m'luchah, nora ka-halachah, s'vivav yom'ru lo. L'cha u-l'cha l'cha ki l'cha, l'cha af l'cha, l'cha Adonai ha-mamlachah, ki lo na'eh, ki lo ya'eh.

Anav bi-m'luchah, podeh ka-halachah, tzaddikav yom'ru lo. L'cha u-l'cha l'cha ki l'cha, l'cha af l'cha, l'cha Adonai ha-mamlachah, ki lo na'eh, ki lo ya'eh.

Kadosh bi-m'luchah, rachum ka-halachah, shin'annav yom'ru lo. L'cha u-l'cha l'cha ki l'cha, l'cha af l'cha, l'cha Adonai ha-mamlachah, ki lo na'eh, ki lo ya'eh.

Takkif bi-m'luchah, tomeich ka-halachah, t'mimav yom'ru lo. L'cha u-l'cha l'cha ki l'cha, l'cha af l'cha, l'cha Adonai ha-mamlachah, ki lo na'eh, ki lo ya'eh.

To God praise belongs, to God praise is due.
Almighty in sovereignty, beloved by right, Your chosen ones sing to You:
Yours only, Yours solely, Yours alone Eternal One is the dominion. To God praise belongs, to God praise is due.
Dominant in sovereignty, Excelling by right, Your Faithful ones sing to You.
Glorious in sovereignty, Hallowed by right, Your Just ones sing to You.
Kindly in sovereignty, Lawgiver by right, Your Ministers sing to You.
None like You in sovereignty, Omnipotent by right, Your People sing to You.
Resplendent in sovereignty, Sovereign by right, Your Thankful ones sing to You.
Unrivalled in sovereignty, Victorious by right, Your Worshippers sing to You.
Worthy of sovereignty, Wonderful by right, Your Witnesses sing to You:
Yours only, Yours solely, Yours alone Eternal One is the dominion.
To God praise belongs, to God praise is due.

The *Seder* concludes on page 50

אַדִּיר הוּא

אַדִּיר הוּא, יִגְאָלֵנוּ בְּקָרוֹב, בִּמְהֵרָה בִּמְהֵרָה, בְּיָמֵינוּ בְקָרוֹב.
אֵל פְּדֵה, אֵל פְּדֵה, פְּדֵה עַמְּךָ בְּקָרוֹב.

בָּחוּר הוּא, גָּדוֹל הוּא, דָּגוּל הוּא, יִגְאָלֵנוּ בְּקָרוֹב, בִּמְהֵרָה בִּמְהֵרָה, בְּיָמֵינוּ בְקָרוֹב.
אֵל פְּדֵה, אֵל פְּדֵה, פְּדֵה עַמְּךָ בְּקָרוֹב.

הָדוּר הוּא, וָתִיק הוּא, זַכַּאי הוּא, יִגְאָלֵנוּ בְּקָרוֹב, בִּמְהֵרָה בִּמְהֵרָה, בְּיָמֵינוּ בְקָרוֹב.
אֵל פְּדֵה, אֵל פְּדֵה, פְּדֵה עַמְּךָ בְּקָרוֹב.

חָסִיד הוּא, טָהוֹר הוּא, יָחִיד הוּא, יִגְאָלֵנוּ בְּקָרוֹב, בִּמְהֵרָה בִּמְהֵרָה, בְּיָמֵינוּ בְקָרוֹב.
אֵל פְּדֵה, אֵל פְּדֵה, פְּדֵה עַמְּךָ בְּקָרוֹב.

כַּבִּיר הוּא, לָמוּד הוּא, מֶלֶךְ הוּא, יִגְאָלֵנוּ בְּקָרוֹב, בִּמְהֵרָה בִּמְהֵרָה, בְּיָמֵינוּ בְקָרוֹב.
אֵל פְּדֵה, אֵל פְּדֵה, פְּדֵה עַמְּךָ בְּקָרוֹב.

נוֹרָא הוּא, סַגִּיב הוּא, עִזּוּז הוּא, יִגְאָלֵנוּ בְּקָרוֹב, בִּמְהֵרָה בִּמְהֵרָה, בְּיָמֵינוּ בְקָרוֹב.
אֵל פְּדֵה, אֵל פְּדֵה, פְּדֵה עַמְּךָ בְּקָרוֹב.

פּוֹדֶה הוּא, צַדִּיק הוּא, קָדוֹשׁ הוּא, יִגְאָלֵנוּ בְּקָרוֹב, בִּמְהֵרָה בִּמְהֵרָה, בְּיָמֵינוּ
בְקָרוֹב. אֵל פְּדֵה, אֵל פְּדֵה, פְּדֵה עַמְּךָ בְּקָרוֹב.

רַחוּם הוּא, שַׁדַּי הוּא, תַּקִּיף הוּא, יִגְאָלֵנוּ בְּקָרוֹב, בִּמְהֵרָה בִּמְהֵרָה, בְּיָמֵינוּ בְקָרוֹב.
אֵל פְּדֵה, אֵל פְּדֵה, פְּדֵה עַמְּךָ בְּקָרוֹב.

Ancient are You, soon may You redeem us, speedily, soon within our lifetime, O God, save; O God, save; save Your people speedily. Blessed are You, Caring are You, Divine are You, Endless are You, Faithful are You, Gracious are You, Holy are You, Infinite are You, Just are You, Kind are You, Loving are You, Mighty are You, Noble are You, One are You, Perfect are You, Righteous are You, Shepherd are You, Teacher are You, Unique are You, Valiant are You, Wise are You, soon may You redeem us, speedily, soon within our lifetime, O God, save; O God, save; save Your people speedily, soon within our lifetime.

Addir hu

Addir hu yig'aleinu b'karov bim'heirah bim'heirah b'yameinu b'karov, eil p'deih, eil p'deih, p'deih ammcha b'karov.

Bachur hu, gadol hu, dagul hu, yig'aleinu b'karov bim'heirah bim'heirah b'yameinu b'karov, eil p'deih, eil p'deih, p'deih ammcha b'karov.

Hadur hu, vatik hu, zakkai hu, yig'aleinu b'karov bim'heirah bim'heirah b'yameinu b'karov, eil p'deih, eil p'deih, p'deih ammcha b'karov.

Chasid hu, tahor hu, yachid hu yig'aleinu b'karov bim'heirah bim'heirah b'yameinu b'karov, eil p'deih, eil p'deih, p'deih ammcha b'karov.

Kabbir hu, lamud hu, melech hu, yig'aleinu b'karov bim'heirah bim'heirah b'yameinu b'karov, eil p'deih, eil p'deih, p'deih ammcha b'karov.

Nora hu, saggiv hu, izzuz hu, yig'aleinu b'karov bim'heirah bim'heirah b'yameinu b'karov, eil p'deih, eil p'deih, p'deih ammcha b'karov.

Podeh hu, tzaddik hu, kadosh hu, yig'aleinu b'karov bim'heirah bim'heirah b'yameinu b'karov, eil p'deih, eil p'deih, p'deih ammcha b'karov.

Rachum hu, shaddai hu, takkif hu, yig'aleinu b'karov bim'heirah bim'heirah b'yameinu b'karov, eil p'deih, eil p'deih, p'deih ammcha b'karov.

The *Seder* concludes on page 50

Siegmund Forst, 1959

אֶחָד מִי יוֹדֵעַ?

אֶחָד מִי יוֹדֵעַ? אֶחָד אֲנִי יוֹדֵעַ: אֶחָד אֱלֹהֵינוּ שֶׁבַּשָּׁמַיִם וּבָאָרֶץ.

Echad mi yodei'a? Echad ani yodei'a. Echad eloheinu she-ba-shamayim u-va'aretz.

שְׁנַיִם מִי יוֹדֵעַ? שְׁנַיִם אֲנִי יוֹדֵעַ: שְׁנֵי לֻחוֹת הַבְּרִית, אֶחָד אֱלֹהֵינוּ שֶׁבַּשָּׁמַיִם וּבָאָרֶץ.

Sh'nayim mi yodei'a? Sh'nayim ani yodei'a. Sh'nei luchot ha-b'rit, echad eloheinu she-ba-shamayim u-va'aretz.

שְׁלֹשָׁה מִי יוֹדֵעַ? שְׁלֹשָׁה אֲנִי יוֹדֵעַ: שְׁלֹשָׁה אָבוֹת, שְׁנֵי לֻחוֹת הַבְּרִית, אֶחָד אֱלֹהֵינוּ שֶׁבַּשָּׁמַיִם וּבָאָרֶץ.

Sh'loshah mi yodei'a? Sh'loshah ani yodei'a. Sh'loshah avot, sh'nei luchot ha-b'rit, echad eloheinu she-ba-shamayim u-va'aretz.

אַרְבַּע מִי יוֹדֵעַ? אַרְבַּע אֲנִי יוֹדֵעַ: אַרְבַּע אִמָּהוֹת, שְׁלֹשָׁה אָבוֹת, שְׁנֵי לֻחוֹת הַבְּרִית, אֶחָד אֱלֹהֵינוּ שֶׁבַּשָּׁמַיִם וּבָאָרֶץ.

Arba mi yodei'a? Arba ani yodei'a. Arba immahot, sh'loshah avot, sh'nei luchot ha-b'rit, echad eloheinu she-ba-shamayim u-va'aretz.

חֲמִשָּׁה מִי יוֹדֵעַ? חֲמִשָּׁה אֲנִי יוֹדֵעַ: חֲמִשָּׁה חֻמְשֵׁי תוֹרָה, אַרְבַּע אִמָּהוֹת, שְׁלֹשָׁה אָבוֹת, שְׁנֵי לֻחוֹת הַבְּרִית, אֶחָד אֱלֹהֵינוּ שֶׁבַּשָּׁמַיִם וּבָאָרֶץ.

Chamishah mi yodei'a? Chamishah ani yodei'a. Chamishah chumshei Torah, arba immahot, sh'loshah avot, sh'nei luchot ha-b'rit, echad eloheinu she-ba-shamayim u-va'aretz.

שִׁשָּׁה מִי יוֹדֵעַ? שִׁשָּׁה אֲנִי יוֹדֵעַ: שִׁשָּׁה סִדְרֵי מִשְׁנָה, חֲמִשָּׁה חֻמְשֵׁי תוֹרָה, אַרְבַּע אִמָּהוֹת, שְׁלֹשָׁה אָבוֹת, שְׁנֵי לֻחוֹת הַבְּרִית, אֶחָד אֱלֹהֵינוּ שֶׁבַּשָּׁמַיִם וּבָאָרֶץ.

Shishah mi yodei'a? Shishah ani yodei'a. Shishah sidrei mishnah, chamishah chumshei Torah, arba immahot, sh'loshah avot, sh'nei luchot ha-b'rit, echad eloheinu she-ba-shamayim u-va'aretz.

שִׁבְעָה מִי יוֹדֵעַ? שִׁבְעָה אֲנִי יוֹדֵעַ: שִׁבְעָה יְמֵי שַׁבַּתָּא, שִׁשָּׁה סִדְרֵי מִשְׁנָה, חֲמִשָּׁה חֻמְשֵׁי תוֹרָה, אַרְבַּע אִמָּהוֹת, שְׁלֹשָׁה אָבוֹת, שְׁנֵי לֻחוֹת הַבְּרִית, אֶחָד אֱלֹהֵינוּ שֶׁבַּשָּׁמַיִם וּבָאָרֶץ.

Shiv'ah mi yodei'a? Shiv'ah ani yodei'a. Shiv'ah y'mei shabbata, shishah sidrei mishnah, chamishah chumshei Torah, arba immahot, sh'loshah avot, sh'nei luchot ha-b'rit, echad eloheinu she-ba-shamayim u-va'aretz.

Who knows one? I know one...
One is our God in heaven and on earth, Two Tablets of the Law, Three Patriarchs, Four Matriarchs, Five Books of Torah, Six Orders of the Mishnah, Seven days of the week. Eight days to circumcision, Nine months to childbirth, Ten Commandments, Eleven stars in Joseph's dream, Twelve Tribes of Israel, Thirteen Attributes of God.

Echad mi yodei'a?

שְׁמוֹנָה מִי יוֹדֵעַ? שְׁמוֹנָה אֲנִי יוֹדֵעַ: שְׁמוֹנָה יְמֵי מִילָה, שִׁבְעָה יְמֵי שַׁבַּתָּא, שִׁשָּׁה סִדְרֵי מִשְׁנָה, חֲמִשָּׁה חֻמְשֵׁי תוֹרָה, אַרְבַּע אִמָּהוֹת, שְׁלֹשָׁה אָבוֹת, שְׁנֵי לֻחוֹת הַבְּרִית, אֶחָד אֱלֹהֵינוּ שֶׁבַּשָּׁמַיִם וּבָאָרֶץ.

Sh'monah mi yodei'a? Sh'monah ani yodei'a. Sh'monah y'mei milah, shiv'ah y'mei shabbata, shishah sidrei mishnah, chamishah chumshai Torah, arba immahot, sh'loshah avot, sh'nei luchot ha-b'rit, echad eloheinu she-ba-shamayim u-va'aretz.

תִּשְׁעָה מִי יוֹדֵעַ? תִּשְׁעָה אֲנִי יוֹדֵעַ: תִּשְׁעָה יַרְחֵי לֵדָה, שְׁמוֹנָה יְמֵי מִילָה, שִׁבְעָה יְמֵי שַׁבַּתָּא, שִׁשָּׁה סִדְרֵי מִשְׁנָה, חֲמִשָּׁה חֻמְשֵׁי תוֹרָה, אַרְבַּע אִמָּהוֹת, שְׁלֹשָׁה אָבוֹת, שְׁנֵי לֻחוֹת הַבְּרִית, אֶחָד אֱלֹהֵינוּ שֶׁבַּשָּׁמַיִם וּבָאָרֶץ.

Tish'ah mi yodei'a? Tish'ah ani yodei'a. Tish'ah yarchei leidah, sh'monah y'mei milah, shiv'ah y'mei shabbata, shishah sidrei mishnah, chamishah chumshei Torah, arba immahot, sh'loshah avot, sh'nei luchot ha-b'rit, echad eloheinu she-ba-shamayim u-va'aretz.

עֲשָׂרָה מִי יוֹדֵעַ? עֲשָׂרָה אֲנִי יוֹדֵעַ: עֲשָׂרָה דִבְּרַיָּא, תִּשְׁעָה יַרְחֵי לֵדָה, שְׁמוֹנָה יְמֵי מִילָה, שִׁבְעָה יְמֵי שַׁבַּתָּא, שִׁשָּׁה סִדְרֵי מִשְׁנָה, חֲמִשָּׁה חֻמְשֵׁי תוֹרָה, אַרְבַּע אִמָּהוֹת, שְׁלֹשָׁה אָבוֹת, שְׁנֵי לֻחוֹת הַבְּרִית, אֶחָד אֱלֹהֵינוּ שֶׁבַּשָּׁמַיִם וּבָאָרֶץ.

Asarah mi yodei'a? Asarah ani yodei'a. Asarah dibraya, tish'ah yarchei leidah, sh'monah y'mei milah, shiv'ah y'mei shabbata, shishah sidrei mishnah, chamishah chumshei Torah, arba immahot, sh'loshah avot, sh'nei luchot ha-b'rit, echad eloheinu she-ba-shamayim u-va'aretz.

אַחַד עָשָׂר מִי יוֹדֵעַ? אַחַד עָשָׂר אֲנִי יוֹדֵעַ: אַחַד עָשָׂר כּוֹכְבַיָּא, עֲשָׂרָה דִבְּרַיָּא, תִּשְׁעָה יַרְחֵי לֵדָה, שְׁמוֹנָה יְמֵי מִילָה, שִׁבְעָה יְמֵי שַׁבַּתָּא, שִׁשָּׁה סִדְרֵי מִשְׁנָה, חֲמִשָּׁה חֻמְשֵׁי תוֹרָה, אַרְבַּע אִמָּהוֹת, שְׁלֹשָׁה אָבוֹת, שְׁנֵי לֻחוֹת הַבְּרִית, אֶחָד אֱלֹהֵינוּ שֶׁבַּשָּׁמַיִם וּבָאָרֶץ.

Achad asar mi yodei'a? Achad asar ani yodei'a. Achad asar kochvayya, asarah dibraya, tish'ah yarchei leidah, sh'monah y'mei milah, shiv'ah y'mei shabbata, shishah sidrei mishnah, chamishah chumshei Torah, arba immahot, sh'loshah avot, sh'nei luchot ha-b'rit, echad eloheinu she-ba-shamayim u-va'aretz.

שְׁנֵים עָשָׂר מִי יוֹדֵעַ? שְׁנֵים עָשָׂר אֲנִי יוֹדֵעַ: שְׁנֵים עָשָׂר שִׁבְטַיָּא, אַחַד עָשָׂר כּוֹכְבַיָּא, עֲשָׂרָה דִבְּרַיָּא, תִּשְׁעָה יַרְחֵי לֵדָה, שְׁמוֹנָה יְמֵי מִילָה, שִׁבְעָה יְמֵי שַׁבַּתָּא, שִׁשָּׁה סִדְרֵי מִשְׁנָה, חֲמִשָּׁה חֻמְשֵׁי תוֹרָה, אַרְבַּע אִמָּהוֹת, שְׁלֹשָׁה אָבוֹת, שְׁנֵי לֻחוֹת הַבְּרִית, אֶחָד אֱלֹהֵינוּ שֶׁבַּשָּׁמַיִם וּבָאָרֶץ.

Sh'neim asar mi yodei'a? Sh'neim asar ani yodei'a. Sh'neim asar shivtayya, achad asar kochvayya, asarah dibraya, tish'ah yarchei leidah, sh'monah y'mei milah, shiv'ah y'mei shabbata, shishah sidrei mishnah, chamishah chumshei Torah, arba immahot, sh'loshah avot, sh'nei luchot ha-b'rit, echad eloheinu she-ba-shamayim u-va'aretz.

This song continues on the next page

שְׁלֹשָׁה עָשָׂר מִי יוֹדֵעַ? שְׁלֹשָׁה עָשָׂר אֲנִי יוֹדֵעַ:
שְׁלֹשָׁה עָשָׂר מִדַּיָּא, שְׁנֵים עָשָׂר שִׁבְטַיָּא, אַחַד
עָשָׂר כּוֹכְבַיָּא, עֲשָׂרָה דִבְּרַיָּא, תִּשְׁעָה יַרְחֵי
לֵדָה, שְׁמוֹנָה יְמֵי מִילָה, שִׁבְעָה יְמֵי שַׁבַּתָּא,
שִׁשָּׁה סִדְרֵי מִשְׁנָה, חֲמִשָּׁה חֻמְשֵׁי תוֹרָה,
אַרְבַּע אִמָּהוֹת, שְׁלֹשָׁה אָבוֹת, שְׁנֵי לֻחוֹת
הַבְּרִית, אֶחָד אֱלֹהֵינוּ שֶׁבַּשָּׁמַיִם וּבָאָרֶץ.

Sh'loshah asar mi yode'a? Shlosh'ah asar ani yode'a. Sh'loshah asar middayya, sh'neim asar shivtayya, achad asar kochvayya, asarah dibraya, tish'ah yarchei leidah, sh'monah y'mei milah, shiv'ah y'mei shabbata, shishah sidrei mishnah, chamishah chumshai Torah, arba immahot, sh'loshah avot, sh'nei luchot ha-b'rit, echad eloheinu she-ba-shamayim u-va'aretz.

Thirteen Attributes of God, Twelve Tribes of Israel, Eleven stars in Joseph's dream, Ten Commandments, Nine months to childbirth, Eight days to circumcision, Seven days of the week, Six Orders of the Mishnah, Five Books of Torah, Four Matriarchs, Three Patriarchs, Two Tablets of the Law. One is our God in heaven and on earth.

An alternative version
(To the tune of 'Green Grow the Rushes-o')

I'll sing you one-o – *Echad mi yodei'a?* What is your one-o?
One is God in heaven and earth and ever more shall be so.

I'll sing you two-o – *Sh'nayim mi yodei'a?* What is your two-o?
Two Tablets of the Law, we'll keep them for evermore, One is God in heaven and earth and ever more shall be so.

I'll sing you three-o – *Sh'loshah mi yodei'a?* What is your three-o?
Three, three the Patriarchs, two Tablets of the Law, we'll keep them for evermore, One is God in heaven and earth and ever more shall be so.

I'll sing you four-o – *Arba mi yodei'a?* What is your four-o?
Four for the Mothers of Israel, three, three the Patriarchs, two Tablets of the Law, we'll keep them for evermore, One is God in heaven and earth and ever more shall be so.

I'll sing you five-o – *Chamishah mi yodei'a?* What is your five-o?
Five for the books of Torah, four for the Mothers of Israel, three, three the Patriarchs, two Tablets of the Law, we'll keep them for evermore, One is God in heaven and earth and ever more shall be so.

I'll sing you six-o – *Shishah mi yodei'a?* What is your six-o?
Six orders of the Mishnah, five for the Books of Torah, four for the Mothers of Israel, three, three the Patriarchs, two Tablets of the Law, we'll keep them for evermore, One is God in heaven and earth and ever more shall be so.

I'll sing you seven-o – *Shiv'ah mi yodei'a?* What is your seven-o?
Seven for the seven days of the week, six orders of the Mishnah, five for the Books of Torah, four for the Mothers of Israel, three, three the Patriarchs, two Tablets of the Law, we'll keep them for evermore, One is God in heaven and earth and ever more shall be so.

I'll sing you eight-o – *Sh'monah mi yodei'a?* What is your eight-o?
Eight days to circumcision, seven for the seven days of the week, six orders of the Mishnah, five for the Books of Torah, four for the Mothers of Israel, three, three the Patriarchs, two Tablets of the Law, we'll keep them for evermore, One is God in heaven and earth and ever more shall be so.

I'll sing you nine-o – *Tish'ah mi yodei'a?* What is your nine-o?
Nine for the months to childbirth, eight days to circumcision, seven for the seven days of the week, six orders of the Mishnah, five for the Books of Torah, four for the Mothers of Israel, three, three the Patriarchs, two Tablets of the Law, we'll keep them for evermore, One is God in heaven and earth and ever more shall be so.

I'll sing you ten-o – *Asarah mi yodei'a?* What is your ten-o?
Ten for the Ten Commandments, nine for the months to childbirth, eight days to circumcision, seven for the seven days of the week, six orders of the Mishnah, five for the Books of Torah, four for the Mothers of Israel, three, three the Patriarchs, two Tablets of the Law, we'll keep them for evermore, One is God in heaven and earth and ever more shall be so.

I'll sing you eleven-o – *Achad asar mi yodei'a?* What is your eleven-o?
Eleven for the stars in Joseph's dream, ten for the Ten Commandments, nine for the months to childbirth, eight days to circumcision, seven for the seven days of the week, six orders of the Mishnah, five for the Books of Torah, four for the Mothers of Israel, three, three the Patriarchs, two Tablets of the Law, we'll keep them for evermore, One is God in heaven and earth and ever more shall be so.

I'll sing you twelve-o – *Sh'neim asar mi yodei'a?* What is your one-o?
Twelve for the tribes of Israel, eleven for the stars in Joseph's dream, ten for the Ten Commandments, nine for the months to childbirth, eight days to circumcision, seven for the seven days of the week, six orders of the Mishnah, five for the Books of Torah, four for the Mothers of Israel, three, three the Patriarchs, two Tablets of the Law, we'll keep them for evermore, One is God in heaven and earth and ever more shall be so.

I'll sing you thirteen-o – *Sh'loshah asar mi yodei'a?* What is your thirteen-o?
Thirteen attributes of God, twelve for the tribes of Israel, eleven for the stars in Joseph's dream, ten for the Ten Commandments, nine for the months to childbirth, eight days to circumcision, seven for the seven days of the week, six orders of the Mishnah, five for the Books of Torah, four for the Mothers of Israel, three, three the Patriarchs, two Tablets of the Law, we'll keep them for evermore, One is God in heaven and earth and ever more shall be so.

The *Seder* concludes on page 50

חַד גַּדְיָא

חַד גַּדְיָא, חַד גַּדְיָא דִּזְבַן אַבָּא בִּתְרֵי זוּזֵי, חַד גַּדְיָא, חַד גַּדְיָא.

Chad gadya, chad gadya dizvan abba bitrei zuzei, chad gadya, chad gadya.

One kid, one kid my father bought for two zuzim.

וְאָתָא שׁוּנְרָא, וְאָכְלָה לְגַדְיָא, דִּזְבַן אַבָּא בִּתְרֵי זוּזֵי, חַד גַּדְיָא, חַד גַּדְיָא.

V'ata shunra, v'achlah l'gadya dizvan abba bitrei zuzei, chad gadya, chad gadya.

Then came a cat and ate the kid my father bought for two zuzim. One kid, one kid.

וְאָתָא כַלְבָּא, וְנָשַׁךְ לְשׁוּנְרָא, דְּאָכְלָה לְגַדְיָא, דִּזְבַן אַבָּא בִּתְרֵי זוּזֵי, חַד גַּדְיָא, חַד גַּדְיָא

V'ata chalba, v'nashach l'shunra, d'achlah l'gadya dizvan abba bitrei zuzei, chad gadya, chad gadya.

Then came a dog and bit the cat that ate the kid my father bought for two zuzim. One kid, one kid.

וְאָתָא חוּטְרָא, וְהִכָּה לְכַלְבָּא, דְּנָשַׁךְ לְשׁוּנְרָא, דְּאָכְלָה לְגַדְיָא, דִּזְבַן אַבָּא בִּתְרֵי זוּזֵי, חַד גַּדְיָא, חַד גַּדְיָא.

V'ata chutra, v'hikkah l'chalba, d'nashach l'shunra, d'achlah l'gadya dizvan abba bitrei zuzei, chad gadya, chad gadya.

Then came a stick and beat the dog that bit the cat that ate the kid my father bought for two zuzim. *Chad gadya, chad gadya.*

וְאָתָא נוּרָא, וְשָׂרַף לְחוּטְרָא, דְּהִכָּה לְכַלְבָּא, דְּנָשַׁךְ לְשׁוּנְרָא, דְּאָכְלָה לְגַדְיָא, דִּזְבַן אַבָּא בִּתְרֵי זוּזֵי, חַד גַּדְיָא, חַד גַּדְיָא.

V'ata nura, v'saraf l'chutra, d'hikkah l'chalba, d'nashach l'shunra, d'achlah l'gadya dizvan abba bitrei zuzei, chad gadya, chad gadya.

Then fire came and burnt the stick that beat the dog that bit the cat that ate the kid my father bought for two zuzim. *Chad gadya, chad gadya.*

וְאָתָא מַיָּא, וְכָבָה לְנוּרָא, דְּשָׂרַף לְחוּטְרָא, דְּהִכָּה לְכַלְבָּא, דְּנָשַׁךְ לְשׁוּנְרָא, דְּאָכְלָה לְגַדְיָא, דִּזְבַן אַבָּא בִּתְרֵי זוּזֵי, חַד גַּדְיָא, חַד גַּדְיָא.

V'ata mayya, v'chavah l'nura, d'saraf l'chutra, d'hikkah l'chalba, d'nashach l'shunra, d'achlah l'gadya dizvan abba bitrei zuzei, chad gadya, chad gadya.

Then water came and quenched the fire that burnt the stick that beat the dog that bit the cat that ate the kid my father bought for two zuzim. *Chad gadya, chad gadya.*

Conclusion

Leader:

Now we have reached the end of our *Seder.* Our thoughts turn for one final time to our ancestors who left Egypt on this night hundreds of years ago. We can now go to sleep peacefully in warmth and safety. For them, the terrifying journey to freedom continued. Let us promise to remember their journey as we celebrate *Pesach* and to do whatever we can in our lives to make sure that no person anywhere in the world is treated like a slave.

All:

We will leave here and remember what our ancestors did and carry the message of freedom for ourselves and future generations.

Chasal siddur pesach k'hilchato

K'chol mishpato v'chukkato

Ka'asher zachinu l'saddeir oto

Kein nizkeh l'fesach le-atid lavo.

Our *Seder* is now completed: we have followed the order, told the story, performed the rites, prayed the prayers and sung the songs. Let us pray for the Passover of the future, when all humanity will live in harmony and peace.

La-shanah ha-ba'ah
bi-y'rushalayim!
Next year in Jerusalem!
La-shanah ha-ba'ah
kol chai nig'al!
Next year in a world
where all are free!

כּוֹס שֶׁל אֱלִיָּהוּ, כּוֹס שֶׁל מִרְיָם

Now that we have given our thanks to God for saving our people from slavery in the past and for giving us freedom in our lives, it is time to look to the future, when all people will live in freedom.

That time is not here yet. According to Jewish tradition, the prophet Elijah will come and tell us when the perfect age of peace and freedom will be here for all humanity. And Miriam the prophet, who guided our people through the wilderness and helped them to find water to keep them alive every day, will give us life and strength to work for the day when Elijah will come to bring that future of perfect peace.

We open the door to welcome Elijah into our *Seder* and into our hearts, and we look for Miriam's support in our everyday lives in the hope that the ideal future we long for will soon be with us.

The door is opened

אֵלִיָּהוּ הַנָּבִיא, אֵלִיָּהוּ הַתִּשְׁבִּי
אֵלִיָּהוּ, אֵלִיָּהוּ, אֵלִיָּהוּ הַגִּלְעָדִי
בִּמְהֵרָה בְיָמֵינוּ יָבוֹא אֵלֵינוּ
עִם בְּשׂוֹרוֹת טוֹבוֹת, יְשׁוּעוֹת וְנֶחָמוֹת.

מִרְיָם הַנְּבִיאָה עֹז וְזִמְרָה בְּיָדָהּ
מִרְיָם תִּרְקוֹד אִתָּנוּ לְהַגְדִּיל זִמְרַת עוֹלָם
בִּמְהֵרָה בְיָמֵינוּ הִיא תְבִיאֵנוּ
אֶל מֵי הַיְשׁוּעָה, אֶל מֵי הַיְשׁוּעָה.

Miriam the prophet, strength and song are in her hand.
Miriam will dance with us to strengthen the world's song.
Soon, and in our time, she will lead us to the waters of salvation.

Leader:
May peace and freedom come to our world soon.

All:
Amen.

The door is closed

The *Seder* concludes with the reading on the next page; some songs from pages 38 to 48 may be sung before concluding

Elijah's Cup, Miriam's Cup

Leader:

One day all people will live in freedom. Just before that day, Elijah the prophet will arrive to tell us it is coming. Let's see if he is here tonight to drink from his cup:

The door is opened

Eliyahu ha-navi, Eliyahu ha-tishbi
Eliyahu, Eliyahu, Eliyahu ha-gil'adi.
Bim'heirah v'yameinu yavo eleinu
Im b'sorot tovot, y'shu'ot v'nechamot.

Miriyam ha-n'vi'ah oz v'zimrah b'yadah
Miriyam tirkod ittanu, l'hagdil zimrat olam.
Bim'herah v'yameinu hi t'vi'einu
El mei ha-y'shu'ah, el mei ha-y'shu'ah

Elijah the prophet, the Tishbite from Gile'ad,
May he come to us soon, in our lifetime,
With tidings of good, of salvation and comfort.

Leader:

May peace and freedom come to our world soon.

All:

Amen.

The door is closed

The *Seder* concludes with the reading on the next page; some songs from pages 38 to 48 may be sung before concluding

בִּרְכַּת הַמָּזוֹן

Afikoman

During the meal, the children can look for the *Afikoman.*

Refill the glasses with wine or grape juice

Thanksgiving for the meal

בָּרוּךְ אֱלֹהֵינוּ שֶׁאָכַלְנוּ מִשֶּׁלוֹ וּבְטוּבוֹ חָיִינוּ. בָּרוּךְ הוּא וּבָרוּךְ שְׁמוֹ.

We have eaten and been satisfied. Help us to be responsive to the needs of others and to listen to their cry for food. Open our eyes and our hearts, so that we may share Your gifts, and help to remove hunger and want from our world.

עֹשֶׂה שָׁלוֹם בִּמְרוֹמָיו, הוּא יַעֲשֶׂה שָׁלוֹם עָלֵינוּ וְעַל כָּל יִשְׂרָאֵל, וְעַל כָּל־בְּנֵי־אָדָם.

Oseh shalom bimromav hu ya'aseh shalom aleinu v'al kol Yisra'el v'al kol b'nei adam.

May the Most High, Source of perfect peace, grant peace to us, to all Israel, and to all humanity.

בָּרוּךְ אַתָּה יְיָ אֱלֹהֵינוּ מֶלֶךְ הָעוֹלָם, בּוֹרֵא פְּרִי הַגָּפֶן.

We thank You, Eternal God, Ruler of the universe, for making the fruit of the vine.

The third glass of wine or grape juice is drunk, leaning to the left

Refill the glasses – including Elijah's – with wine or grape juice.
A cup of water for Miriam may also be filled at this point.

Once more we give our thanks to God for bringing our ancestors to freedom. As we say a final *halleluyah*, let us recognise that the best way to show how grateful we are is to do whatever we can to help those who still live in slavery.

הַלְלוּיָהּ!

Repeat the blessing for wine, then drink the fourth glass of wine or grape juice, leaning to the left

(pages 24-30, 32, 33, 36)

Thanksgiving for the Meal

Afikoman

During the meal, the children can look for the *Afikoman*.

Refill the glasses with wine or grape juice

Leader:
Let us thank God for the meal we have just eaten. When we finish, we'll have another drink to help us to give thanks.

Baruch eloheinu she-achalnu mi-shelo u-v'tuvo chayyinu. Baruch hu u-varuch sh'mo.

We thank You God for giving us food to eat which keeps us alive. Let God be praised.

Leader:
We are lucky that we have enough food to eat.

All:
We promise to remember those in our world who are hungry and try to share God's gifts equally.

Baruch atah Adonai eloheinu melech ha-olam borei p'ri ha-gafen.

We thank You God, for making the fruit of the vine.

The third glass of wine or grape juice is drunk, leaning to the left

Leader:
Now we're going to give our thanks to God for one final time by singing or shouting out the word that praises God! Then we'll have our final drink of the *Seder* in celebration of our freedom.

Repeat the blessing for wine, then drink the fourth glass of wine or grape juice, leaning to the left

פֶּסַח, מַצָּה, וּמָרוֹר

רַבָּן גַּמְלִיאֵל הָיָה אוֹמֵר, "כָּל שֶׁלֹּא אָמַר
שְׁלֹשָׁה דְבָרִים אֵלּוּ בַּפֶּסַח, לֹא יָצָא יְדֵי
חוֹבָתוֹ, וְאֵלּוּ הֵן, פֶּסַח, מַצָּה, וּמָרוֹר."

Rabban Gamliel used to say; 'If, on the Passover, you do not explain these three things, you have not fulfilled your obligation: ***Pesach***, ***Matzah*** and ***Maror***.'

Pesach **– the Passover sacrifice**
The bone on the ***Seder*** plate reminds us of the lamb that our ancestors would offer to God at this time of the year. *Pesach* is a spring festival and a lamb is a symbol of the spring. Because animal sacrifice ended when the Temple was destroyed, we just have the bone to remind us of this ancient practice.

Matzah **– unleavened bread**
According to the story in the Bible, the people leaving Egypt were in a hurry and did not have time to wait for the dough to rise before making bread – so when they baked it, they made *Matzah*. Eating *Matzah* during *Pesach* is another way of remembering the experiences of the people who left Egypt.

בָּרוּךְ אַתָּה יְיָ אֱלֹהֵינוּ מֶלֶךְ הָעוֹלָם, הַמּוֹצִיא לֶחֶם מִן הָאָרֶץ.

We praise You, Eternal God, Ruler of the Universe: You cause wheat to grow from the earth to enable us to make bread.

בָּרוּךְ אַתָּה יְיָ אֱלֹהֵינוּ מֶלֶךְ הָעוֹלָם, אֲשֶׁר קִדְּשָׁנוּ
בְּמִצְוֹתָיו, וְצִוָּנוּ עַל אֲכִילַת מַצָּה.

We praise You, Eternal God, Ruler of the universe: Your commandments make us special and You ask us to eat *Matzah.*

Lean to the left and eat a piece of *Matzah*

Maror **– bitter herbs**
We eat the *Maror* to make us realise how bitter the lives of our people were when the Egyptians made them work so hard as slaves. It should also remind us how important it is that we do whatever we can to make sure that there are no slaves in our world. Let's take some bitter herbs along with some charoset and get ready to eat them:

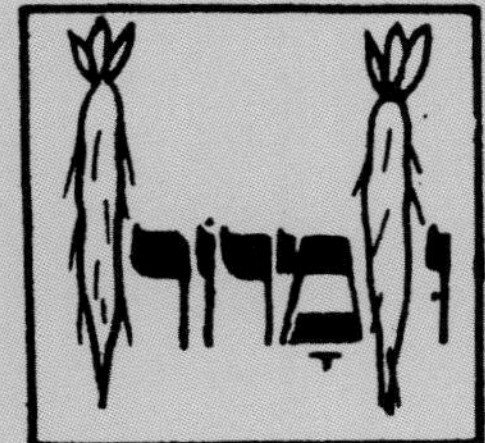

בָּרוּךְ אַתָּה יְיָ אֱלֹהֵינוּ מֶלֶךְ הָעוֹלָם, אֲשֶׁר קִדְּשָׁנוּ בְּמִצְוֹתָיו,
וְצִוָּנוּ עַל אֲכִילַת מָרוֹר.

We praise You, Eternal God, Ruler of the universe: Your commandments make us special and You ask us to eat bitter herbs.

All eat a piece of *Maror* –Now it's time to eat our meal!

(pages 21, 22, 23)

The Seder plate

Leader:
There are lots of things on the *Seder* table to make us ask questions about *Pesach*. We should try to find answers to help us remember how our people left Egypt and how important it is that all people can enjoy freedom.

***Karpas* – parsley**
We have already eaten this but it's another reminder of spring – and the salt water that we dip it in makes us think of our people's tears when they were made to work as slaves.

Pesach
The bone and the egg remind us of the spring sacrifices our people used to take to the Temple in Jerusalem at this time of year.

Matzah
This unleavened bread that we eat for the next seven days reminds us that our people had to leave Egypt in a hurry.

Baruch atah Adonai eloheinu melech ha-olam ha-motzi lechem min ha-aretz

We thank You, God, for letting the earth give us bread.

Baruch atah Adonai eloheinu melech ha-olam asher kidd'shanu b'mitzvotav v'tzivvanu al achilat Matzah.

We thank You God, for Your rules that make us special and for asking us to eat *Matzah.*

Lean to the left and eat a piece of *Matzah*

Maror
The bitter herbs make us think of the bitter times our people had when they were slaves in Egypt. We take some bitter herbs and dip them in *Charoset,* the sweet paste that reminds us of the bricks our people made.

Baruch atah Adonai eloheinu melech ha-olam asher kidd'shanu b'mitzvotav v'tzivvanu al achilat Maror.

We thank You God, for Your rules that make us special and for asking us to eat *Maror.*

All eat a piece of *Maror* –Now it's time to eat real food!

הַלֵּל

How grateful we are, then, that God has given us all these things – and so many more! We give thanks to God who did all these wonderful things for our ancestors and for us.

God has led us:
from slavery to freedom;
from sadness to joy;
from mourning to celebration;
from darkness to light;
Let us sing a new song to God:
Halleluyah!

הַלְלוּ הַלְלוּ הַלְלוּ
כֹּל הַנְּשָׁמָה תְּהַלֵּל יָהּ, הַלְלוּ הַלְלוּיָהּ.

We give our thanks to God by drinking our second glass of wine or grape juice:

2 בָּרוּךְ אַתָּה יְיָ אֱלֹהֵינוּ מֶלֶךְ הָעוֹלָם, בּוֹרֵא פְּרִי הַגָּפֶן

We thank You, Eternal God, Ruler of the universe, for making the fruit of the vine.

The second glass of wine or grape juice is drunk, leaning to the left

(pages 18, 19, 20)

Hallel

Leader:

Our people were free! They were so happy, they sang songs of praise to God who had saved them. One of the Hebrew words for praising God is ***Halleluyah***!

Hallelu hallelu hallelu, hallelu, halleluyah!
Kol ha-n'shamah t'hallel yah, hallelu halleluyah!
Let us give praise – Let us all praise God. *Halleluyah!*

All:

Let's have our second drink to show how happy we are for the things God did for our people and for us:

Baruch atah Adonai eloheinu melech ha-olam borei p'ri ha-gafen.

We thank You God, for making the fruit of the vine.

The second glass of wine or grape juice is drunk, leaning to the left